A SMITHSONIAN NATURE BOOK

Redwings

ROBERT W. NERO

Smithsonian Institution Press, Washington, D.C.

1984

Front cover: Male Redwing song-spread display in an apple tree.
(Douglas G. Smith)

Back cover: The author on a May morning, 1982, placing a
mounted male "dummy" in Redwing territory.
(Robert R. Taylor)

Library of Congress Cataloging in Publication Data

Nero, Robert W.
Redwings.

(A Smithsonian nature book)
Bibliography: p.
Includes index.
1. Red-winged blackbird. I. Title. II. Series.
QL696.P2475N46 1983   598.8'81   83–10486
ISBN 0–87474–676–0
ISBN 0–87474–677–9(paper)

The paper in this book meets the guidelines for permanence
and durability of the Committee on Production Guidelines
for Book Longevity of the Council on Library Resources.

Dedicated to my wife, Ruth F. Nero

Contents

A relaxed male Redwing rests in a willow. Note that the red wing patch is almost concealed. In territorial display and courtship, these red patches are prominently displayed, and they are always visible when the birds are in flight. (Fred W. Lahrman)

An adult female Redwing, about two-thirds the size of the male, appears in the spring as a black-and-white-streaked bird, with brown above. The amount of red pigment in the female plumage seems to increase with age. (Bruce Lyon)

A male Yellow-headed Blackbird, another member of the Icteridae family, in phragmites. (Dennis Fast)

A male Redwing gives a sexual display. (Dale Paulson)

This male is giving an intensive display to its mate. (Andrew M. Lindsay)

A male Redwing on a cattail head delivers a primary song. Note the raised epaulet. (Douglas G. Smith)

Young nestlings gape for food. (Hamilton Greenwood)

A female Redwing feeds one of five nestlings—all gaping and stretching to be fed. (Andrew M. Lindsay)

Out of the nest! A fledgling with downy head-tufts bristles with developing feathers. (Hamilton Greenwood)

This is part of a large flock of Red-winged Blackbirds over a cornfield in the fall. (Robert R. Taylor)

Foreword

It is about time that Bob Nero with all of his eloquence wrote a book about Red-winged Blackbirds. Through his detailed studies of blackbird behavior, beginning in Wisconsin and extending to Saskatchewan and Manitoba, Bob accumulated a lot of biological knowledge that needed to be on paper. He started by writing several scientific papers but procrastinated on putting all of the details together in a popular version. Whenever he heard the song "Bye, Bye, Blackbird" or reminisced about university days, he would always conclude through tearful eyes that he should write a book about blackbirds (Bob is no stranger to writing books about other things such as Great Gray Owls and cougars). With some prodding from colleagues and friends, and much encouragement from the Smithsonian Institution Press, Bob has completed a book that has been a career in the making but took only a few months to write. This is the book that he should have written first since blackbirds have been so dear to his heart.

If you wanted to know something about the problems and techniques whereby wildlife managers and farmers have tried to manage blackbirds in order to scare them or to control their numbers, then this is the book for you. You will enjoy learning many new things about the territorial and courtship behavior of a bird that is often common but little known, as Bob Nero tells you about "Redwings."

Merlin W. Shoesmith, Ph.D.
Head, Biological Services
Wildlife Branch
Manitoba Department of Natural Resources
Winnipeg, Manitoba

Preface

Much of this book is based on my own published material, drawn from my thesis of the mid-fifties, and in a few cases from original field notes. I have mostly written about what I know best, namely, the behavior of Redwings during the breeding season. Where it seemed feasible and worthwhile, I have included excerpts from the literature of the past three decades, although so much research has been carried out on the Redwing that this has been difficult to do.

Over the years, the Redwing has been the subject of numerous studies. Thomas Nuttall gave it six pages in his 1832 monograph and Audubon devoted six pages to the species in 1834 in his *Birds of America*. The earliest in-depth study, conducted by Arthur A. Allen, was an eighty-six page treatise published in 1914. Allen took a broad ecological approach, relating vegetational growth and food species to seasonal behavior of Redwings around Ithaca, New York. His report provides a permanent source of information on breeding biology and adaptation to environment. Gene H. Linford carried out a substantial and sound behavior study of the Redwing in Utah for a master's thesis in 1935. Together with accounts of subspecies, Arthur C. Bent (1958) provides fifty-six pages of material on the species. Several dozen authorities from across the country contributed to this volume of the Bent "Life Histories" series, a compilation made possible, after Bent's death in 1954, by a dedicated group of ornithologists led by Wendell Taber. The book, as is true of all the others in the Bent series, remains a basic source of detailed information.

On the basis of a Red-winged Blackbird bibliography by Noel Cutright (1973) and a computer print-out of Redwing publications for the period 1972 to 1980, I discovered that there have been more than seven hundred studies in whole or part on Redwings since Audubon favored the bird with his attention. In the century from 1800 to 1899, there were four papers; 1900–25, thirteen; 1926–50, sixty-eight; 1951–60, forty-six; 1961–70, two hundred twenty-six; 1971–80, three hundred forty-nine!

In some respects the Red-winged Blackbird, at least among wild birds, has become an ornithological white rat, and is now the subject of an ever-increasing number of studies. For example, some highly technical studies of Redwing physiology and endocrine (hormone-producing) systems have been carried out. Publications on functions of the brain, including a search for vocalization areas, are not unlike some mammalian studies. In one case, there was even a comparative study of certain liver enzymes in Redwings and white rats. These studies have appeared in appropriate technical journals such as *Acta Zoologica, Pharmacologist,* and *Brain Research Bulletin.* I made no effort to obtain these reports and have not listed them in the Bibliography.

I find it impressive that there have been seventy-five masters' or doctorate theses on the Redwing. Although basic biological, natural history, and ecological aspects are found throughout this body of work, there has been a small explosion of studies related directly or indirectly to two major problems originating with the Red-winged Blackbird and other "blackbirds," for example, the Common Grackle. These are the agricultural pest and control aspects (more than two hundred articles) and large winter roosts (forty-seven items). These two subjects are dealt with in chapter 11. There are many additional titles listed on these subjects in bibliographies available from the U.S. Fish and Wildlife Service, Bird Damage Control Section, Denver, Colorado. Because of overlap in citations between material from this latter source and the bibliography by Cutright, I found it too cumbersome to attempt to sort out the blackbird studies reported therein.

Professor Gordon H. Orians and his students at the University of Washington have produced some serious and thoughtful reports. Orians stands out as the individual who has contributed the most over a long period of time. He was a fellow graduate student with me at Madison, also working with Professor John T. Emlen, Jr. I have looked carefully at Orians's 1980 study, *Some Adaptations of Marsh-nesting Blackbirds,* which is a very advanced ecological report, closely relating birds, environment, and adaptations, with considerable emphasis on the Red-winged Blackbird. I found it hard going but thought-provoking. Beyond Orians, however, it becomes rather subjective how one chooses from among the many other researchers who have made substantial contributions to Redwing literature (including all those students who have produced theses). Their names and their works appear, to the extent that I have used their material, in the Bibliography, and specific references are cited in the Notes.

But this is intended to be a popular book on the Redwing, not a technical paper or a complete survey of the Redwing literature. Rather, I have attempted to provide a stimulating and enjoyable guide to the Redwing's major activities as observed by myself and others.

A delightful and pleasant brief outline of much Red-winged Blackbird behavior may be found in *A Guide to the Behavior of Common Birds* by Donald W. Stokes (Little, Brown, 1979). Eight pages in a separate chapter are devoted to this species. Thus, there should be no doubt that the Redwing is indeed one of the most familiar birds in North America.

Acknowledgments

I would like to thank Maurice L. Giltz, Vene Parnell, Mary Ann Rodewald, Carol F. Smith, and Patrick J. Weatherhead for helpful reviews and criticisms of the manuscript. Carol Smith, in particular, offered many useful comments on the entire manuscript. Pat Weatherhead provided a good perspective from the critical viewpoint of an active Red-winged Blackbird researcher, and he also reviewed the final draft.

This book owes its existence to the incentive supplied by Edward F. "Ted" Rivinus, who suggested I undertake the preparation of a second book for the Smithsonian Institution Press. When I said I thought I could possibly do something on the Red-winged Blackbird, it was Ted, Director Emeritus, SIP, who said: "Good. Now get started." I am grateful for his confidence in me and for his having urged me to write the book. Immeasurable assistance was received from Hope Pantell, editor for the Smithsonian Institution Press, who steered the manuscript with her fine judgment through its final stages.

Assistance was supplied in various ways by L. David Beletsky, Jerome F. Besser, Fred J. Brenner, David E. Davis, Harry A.G. Harris, Irene Hamerton, Donald J. Haugen, Ruth L. Hine, Janet Hinshaw, Larry C. Holcomb, Francis C. James, Robert E. Jones, Don L. Keith, James Larson, Tom McHugh, Brooke Meanley, Helen Molet, Gordon H. Orians, Ralph S. Palmer, Frank W. Peek, and Shirley Rutledge.

I am especially indebted to Wally Fuchs who drafted the maps and figures, and to James Carson for the delightful sketches which add so much to the book.

Betty Struthers assisted me with the arduous task of proof reading the manuscript and the galleys. Typing of an early draft was done by Barbara C. Bean; the final draft was typed by Nancy D. Markus. I am also indebted to Irene Hamerton, who provided capable assistance in the preparation of the Index.

I owe special thanks to the Manitoba Department of Natural Resources for support in writing the book, and would like especially to thank Richard C. Goulden, Director of the Wildlife Branch, and Merlin W. Shoesmith, Head of Biological Services. I am also indebted to the latter for the gracious foreword to the book.

I could hardly have written the book without the encouragement of John T. Emlen Jr.; as my major advisor and a professor in the University of Wisconsin Zoology Department, John Emlen guided my Red-winged Blackbird studies from 1948 to 1955. He also served in an important way during those years as a father figure. I am grateful to him and his wife for their interest in me and the welfare of my family.

No family has suffered more anguish and uncertainty as a consequence of a husband and father's involvement in writing than mine. My general irritability during many weekend sessions ruined many otherwise fine days. I apologize and ask my family's forgiveness. This applies particularly to my wife.

Introduction

One way of beginning a book about the Red-winged Blackbird, or Redwing, is to tell something about the author and his involvement with the subject. In this case, my personal life overlaps so thoroughly that it is difficult to think of certain years without thinking of Redwings. For a number of years they were my major preoccupation.

I first started looking seriously at the Red-winged Blackbird in 1948 while a graduate student at the University of Wisconsin. A two-and-one-quarter acre cattail marsh adjacent to the southeast corner of Lake Wingra, Wisconsin, and about three miles south of the Madison campus, was my main study area from 1948 to 1953. Although I have watched Redwings every year since, never again has it been with the intensity of those early years. At any time now, driving along a highway, the sight of Redwings on territory in roadside marshes evokes a galaxy of Redwing behavior. And their melodious song, whenever I first hear it, tells me it's spring. Even in traffic with the car radio on and conversation flowing, my ears prick up at that song, forever a part of my long association with this species.

One spring, when I was thirteen or fourteen years old, I found a single male Redwing by a small pond, with some willows and cattails at one end, near my rural Milwaukee home. The site was surrounded by many acres of open farmland. When the bird hovered above me, I sent it higher still by waving a cattail stalk at it, but it wouldn't go away. I don't suppose I realized that the bird was "on territory." As far as I can remember that was my first close contact with this species. But even at that moment, I enjoyed the way it stayed by the pond, content to see it up close, and glad to feel its response when I waved it off. There would be the agonies of adolescence and a war in the interim between that event and a time when Redwings would be foremost on my mind.

As a graduate student it was my good fortune to be invited to assist the late James R. Beer with a Red-winged Blackbird study he and Douglas Tibbitts were carrying out while Jim was working toward a Ph.D. thesis on muskrats at the Lake Wingra Marsh. It didn't take me long to decide. The marsh sounded like the place for me, offering solitude and field experience. Jim Beer convinced me that I could gather enough additional information on Redwings for a thesis. And that's how it all began.

John T. Emlen, Jr., my major professor, agreed to the project, and at his suggestion I spent much of the first spring observing and recording the behavior of one territorial male. To stand and watch a single bird, hour after hour, day after day; its own behavior, interactions with other males and other species, all carefully recorded in this first lesson in watching birds—it was a revelation. My typed notes indicate that I called it "Beer's Marsh," and well I might, for often when I was watching "my bird" I could hear Jim splashing through the marsh. I still recall seeing his brawny figure trudging up a steep sidewalk on campus, wearing hip waders nonchalantly rolled halfway down, khaki pants (we all wore some portion of military clothing then) and a T-shirt, a dead muskrat dangling by the tail in each brown fist. Beer was working on muskrat physiology so it was not unusual for him to carry dead 'rats across campus.

Many of the techniques of trapping and color-banding Redwings I learned from Jim Beer. I tried to imitate his energetic approach to his project, his unconcern for personal appearance while working, and his dedication to research. I was impressed by his technical articles, several of which he thrust into my hands. Suddenly I was part of the challenging world of research, a young ornithologist in the making.

Busy as I was with classes, I am reminded by my notes that I was at the marsh almost every day, starting March 22, 1948. Early spring was a time when male Redwings were busy establishing territorial boundaries. I still have detailed maps showing the movements of my bird, with the length of time it spent at each position. The maps covered many hours, and included much material not directly used in my thesis, but useful in leading me to an understanding and appreciation of Redwings.

Redwings, it turned out, were not just scattered randomly across the marsh; rather, the males moved within definite systems. I had no idea things were so formalized. What I had earlier perceived as a marsh ringing with the sounds of exuberant birdlife turned out to be a tense, regulated series of actions and reactions—compelling, structured, and effective. Even today, when I stand by a marsh, I am aware of the intensity of interactions that move Redwings and other birds back and forth, or force them into a showy display of plumage and heightened song. The ties that bind these birds together are firm and relentless.

At the peak of activity on a spring morning the pace is frenetic. I was barely able to scribble notes fast enough to keep up with the action. It seems bedlam—until one sorts it out. And that was my role: to watch these Redwings closely over a long period of time, and, eventually, make some sense of all their madcap activity.

Several days after my vigil began, the first female Redwings ar-

rived, initiating a great burst of activities, all of which I tried to describe in my increasingly frantic notes. By late April I had observed
courtship and mating, and my notes are embellished with little
sketches of male and female displays. My own courtship was proceed-
ing at about the same time. In mid-June I married a girl I first met on
a streetcar in downtown Milwaukee. Ruth became my diligent assistant.

That first summer my wife and I daily pedalled our bicycles (we
had no car) three miles from the campus to the marsh, leaving before
dawn to set traps for Redwings. I was determined to color-band as
many birds as possible in order to better understand their behavior.
We carried hip waders, binoculars, notebooks, banding equipment, and
stale baked goods for bait (white bread is still the best bait I know for
trapping Redwings, and I'm told that this also applies to grackles).
Ruth spent her time tending traps in a nearby park while I worked in
the marsh. Occasionally we nibbled on a sweetroll or glazed doughnut
from our bait supply, but otherwise we hurriedly returned to the married couples' residence on the campus, arriving back just in time for
the final call to breakfast. Usually we sped into the cafeteria wearing
our scruffy field clothing, bits of cattail fluff in our hair, to save time
or to show that we were doing "field work."

Throughout those Redwing years I worked for the Zoology Department Museum, collecting and preparing bird and mammal specimens. Friends and colleagues from that period will doubtless recall the
long hours my wife and I spent in the dark little basement room in
Birge Hall, which then housed the research collections and the preparation area. I'm sure Ruth will never forget the many tedious hours
she spent down there snipping and scraping fat from waterfowl skins,
a task she faced with no complaint. Additional monies were obtained
one year by assisting John Emlen with a survey of rats on campus
(they were numerous in the Agriculture Department's farm buildings).

In 1952 I was the proud recipient of a Louis Agassiz Fuertes Research Grant for $100. It was a sum and an honor greatly appreciated. Additional support came from unusual sources. For instance, Tom McHugh, an Emlen student, working part-time for Disney Studios, once paid me seventy-five cents each for fifty live House Sparrows, which I captured by prowling about the rafters above steaming cattle in their stalls on the Agricultural campus. Flashlight in one hand, I quickly grabbed the protesting birds with the other hand and stuffed them into a bag; being careful, meanwhile, to watch my footing. Later, those birds were released from a metal cage as a prairie fire set by McHugh overswept them. In the widely shown Disney film *The Vanishing Prairie*, small birds flit upward through the smoke of a raging prairie fire—my seventy-five-cent sparrows aloft forever!

Another summer, I worked for three weeks as special assistant to Wallace Kirkland, a *LIFE* magazine photographer. I searched through a small, marshy pond at the Madison Fish Hatchery, bringing odd animals for Kirkland to photograph. I enthusiastically interpreted Redwing behavior for him, urging him to capture their displays on film. Later, I was pleased to see a chapter in a book he wrote that included a section on Red-winged Blackbirds. The book, called *Recollections of a LIFE Photographer*, made me feel proud, for it mentioned my studies.

By the end of my first field year, 1948, Redwing behavior seemed fairly easy to follow, but each year thereafter brought more puzzles, and especially more exceptions to patterns of behavior as I knew them. By 1953, most early "rules" of behavior had been broken. I was left with a bundle of field notes and records that indicated considerable individual variation. One of the professors on my thesis committee later suggested that I was over-emphasizing "abnormal behavior." Surely there must be something that they all do in the same way? Yes, but birds do show a great deal of individual behavior, and the longer I watched Redwings the more of this I saw. I suspect this is so for all species. Only in short-term studies are behavior patterns simple and regular.

In the spring of 1955, I had access to the Zoology Department's new telephoto lens and a camera, so for a few weeks I focused on photographic work. Yet, I was photographing Redwings with insight into their behavior. I chose subjects obviously involved in a specific stage of the breeding sequence as performers, or elicited response at times with mounted ("stuffed") birds or dummies, thus getting my subjects to behave within good camera range.

Shortly after I got my Ph.D. degree, my family and I moved from Madison to Regina, the capital of Saskatchewan, where I had a job as assistant director of the province's new museum of natural history. It was a long hot trip from Madison to Regina, and we made few casual stops. It seemed a strange coincidence that I should come across a road-killed aberrant adult male Red-winged Blackbird. The bird was lying on the road shoulder near some marshland. It looked fresh, so, despite heavy traffic, I pulled over to have a look. Even as I picked it up I could see that it was an unusual specimen, one worth writing about—two vestigial wing claws protruded from the feathers on both wings, small, grayish, horny growths readily visible along the wings' leading edges. It turned out to be the first record of a passerine bird with this condition in North America.

In 1956 I decided to study the Yellow-headed Blackbird, to compare its behavior with that of the Redwing and other blackbirds. (There was a good colony of Yellowheads at a marsh within the city limits, close to where I worked.) It was my good fortune to work in the field with Fred W. Lahrman, a fellow employee of the museum. Fred was (and is) an experienced and extremely skillful artist-taxidermist-photographer. Although he had not previously used a motion-picture camera, his first efforts at capturing the behavior of Yellowheads and Redwings on film were superb, and we spent many happy hours together. The original, silent version of this film was shown at the American Ornithologists' Union annual meeting in Regina in 1959. When the image first came on the screen it was both upside down and backward. I spent a long ten minutes at the podium while the film was rewound—twice. After the morning session, Ralph Palmer, well-known ornithologist and editor of the "Handbook of North American Birds" series, commented on my performance as follows: "Well, Nero" (shaking my hand) "you may not be much of an ornithologist, but you're a damned good ad libber!"

That film, titled "Marsh Blackbirds," was finally completed and produced with a full-length sound track in 1976 (with the assistance [and budget] of Donald G. Keith, Manitoba Department of Natural Resources, where I went to work in 1970). To date, more than thirty copies have been sold across Canada, the United States, and in Europe.

The TV staff at Brandon (population 38,000), Manitoba, brought my affair with the Redwing to a peak. Previewing the film, including mating episodes, the staff decided it "wasn't quite suitable for public showing." The film was returned, unused. For several days people in the Manitoba Wildlife Branch laughed over the fact that the Redwing film had been banned in Brandon!

Renewed Contact with Redwings

Working for a few days with photographer Bob Taylor in May 1982, trying to get color photos of Redwings for this book, provided me with a renewed intimate contact with these birds. One particular situation was memorable. As usual, we were operating without a blind, for Redwings are bold birds and a lot of behavior can be elicited with dummies at close range. As I stood on the edge of cattails at a small pond, reflecting on the three decades that had passed since I first began looking at Redwings, the dummy I was using—a mounted male with spread tail and well-exposed epaulets, an aggressive pose—drew a quick response from a well-established male. "Song-spread" display, first at a distance, then within a few feet, with fast little flashes of "bill-tilting," eventually led him to direct attack—a pounce on the back with a fierce peck and off again, all this only a few yards in front of us.

This male had two females on his territory. One was well settled and mostly remained out of sight at the far end of the male's territory. The second female acted as if she had only arrived a short time earlier. She was restless, chattered noisily, thus eliciting aggressive behavior from the male, which flew at her with a dive and fierce "growl." Eventually, she left the marsh to perch in some oak trees a few dozen yards from the marsh. Thus the male was faced with two strong stimulus sources: the mounted male fastened to a cattail in his territory and the female in the trees. Repeatedly, the male, worn from grappling with the immovable intruder, would start to fly toward the noisy female in the trees, then midway in flight he would swerve, hesitate, and return to confront the dummy. It was remarkable to see the way in which the male was drawn off course as he commenced his flight, each time slowing, then pulling back to the battle. It was as if upon suddenly seeing the dummy from a new angle the full effect of this stimulus source was renewed. During this same period of observation the male occasionally interrupted this sequence to give full sexual display, responding to the calls of his first mate, but always screened by cattails or out of camera range.

As a romantic (less a civil servant than a frustrated poet), I tend to be generous in some of my viewpoints regarding bird behavior. Some of my colleagues might feel that I err in attributing certain meaning to behavior that could be explained in simpler terms. Mostly, I play it safe, taking the role of observer involved in descriptive natural history, trying valiantly not to let my biases intrude, but still they do. True, I see birds as fairly dynamic entities, capable of split-second changes in mood and showing varied responses with time and place. I admit to believing, for example, that Redwings are capable of fine discernment, showing a high degree of individual recognition, and even levels of perception. In my use of dummies to elicit behavior (usually of a predetermined type, the result of observations in a more natural situation), I have never been convinced that the responding birds "believed" that the dummies were alive. I think that they are simply responding to strong three-dimensional stimuli, varying in strength with their own internal state and the multiple facets of surrounding stimulus sources. These latter are exceedingly diverse—a bird is almost always surrounded by a multiplicity of interacting factors. Yet I have willingly used dummies to elicit behavior that I strongly believe is largely usable (e.g., serves as a source of photographs or provides a finer view of what has been only glimpsed) and is altogether a part of a bird's behavioral repertoire.

Ecologist F. Fraser Darling said in 1946: "In some instances I feel that the most simple explanation of an act of behaviour is to follow the bare outline of our own mental processes in such a situation. I believe the teleological approach to animal behaviour to be dangerous, but the current objection to anthropomorphism can be overdone. . . . The organism is a functional unity related both to its past and its future, and at any one moment presents but a phase of its life history."

My close observations of Redwings have brought me a new perception of birds in general. In spring, everywhere I go I see birds performing their rituals of courtship, raising their wings, tipping and bowing, each in its special way. All this has enriched my life, and I here happily share my knowledge of Redwings in the hope of helping others attain new delights in understanding and observing this beautiful and common bird.

1

A Family of Birds

Found across the continent in habitats varying from coastal salt marshes to prairie sloughs and upland meadows, the Red-winged Blackbird, with its striking color pattern and distinctive song, is a familiar species to many people. Commonplace, bold, and colorful, the male of this species—its black plumage set off by red "shoulder" patches—is surely one of the best-known birds in North America. Red-winged Blackbird is the Redwing's official name. In the past it has been known as the Swamp Blackbird, Marsh Blackbird, Red-winged Starling, Red-shouldered Starling, Red-winged Oriole, and Red-shoul-dered Blackbird. The name Redwing is in common use today and I have used it in this book. (It should not be confused with a Eurasian thrush properly called the Redwing and well known in the British Isles.)

The Redwing's scientific name is *Agelaius phoeniceus*. *Agelaius* (pronounced "a ge li' us") comes from the Greek agelaios, meaning "belonging to a flock," a reference to its social habits. The specific name *phoeniceus* (pronounced "foy ne' ke us" or "fe ni' -se us") is de-rived from the Latin word for purple-red, a color known in classical times as Phoenician or Tyrian purple. Note that the names are chiefly descriptive of the male of the species; the female Redwing is not as well known. About two-thirds the size of the male, this lovely bird appears in spring as a black-and-white-streaked bird, brown above. Jon-athon Dwight noted in 1900 that "a pinkish or salmon tinge is often found . . . especially about the chin and head and an orange or crimson tinge may show on the 'shoulders' of the older birds."

Working some years ago with color-banded birds, I verified that younger females have a yellowish tinge on the throat and no red on the epaulets (as indicated by Dwight) and thus can be readily identi-fied from older birds. The amount of red pigment in the female plu-mage apparently increases with the bird's age, some females becoming quite colorful. A subspecies in Utah is largely marked by an increased amount of red plumage of the throat area and epaulets of females (and brighter red in the males).

The Red-winged Blackbird is a member of the family Icteridae, a group including such diverse forms as grackles, orioles, and meadow-larks. This interesting family includes many orioles of the genus *Icte-rus* (a term derived from a Greek word for a yellow-green bird), hence its scientific name. A common name for this group, the "Troupial" family, is from the French "troupe," a reference to their habit of flocking. The family Icteridae is found only in the Western Hemisphere, and occurs in North, Central, and South America and the West Indies. The "Blackbird" of the European continent and England—the one that was "baked in a pie"—is an unrelated species of thrush, a close cousin of the American Robin.

There are ninety-four species in the Icteridae family, the majority of them found in South America. About twenty members of the family inhabit North America. These are the Bobolink; Eastern and Western Meadowlarks; Yellow-headed, Red-winged, Tricolored, Rusty, and Brewer's Blackbirds; Boat-tailed and Common Grackles; Brown-headed and Bronzed Cowbirds; Orchard, Black-headed, Scott's, Hooded, Northern (comprised of the former Baltimore and Bullock's Oriole now merged as one species), Lichtenstein's, and Spotted-breasted Orioles.

There is a preponderance of black plumage among these birds— this is typical of the group. In those that are wholly black, the Common Grackle and Brewer's Blackbird, for example, there is a bluish gloss or iridescence to much of the plumage, especially on the head and neck feathers. Among the others, yellow, red, or orange colors are common. In studying albinism in the Redwing I discovered that in the adult male there is a pinkish-orange cast to the feathers of the head, neck, and breast concealed beneath the black pigmentation. Whenever the black pigment melanin was missing, owing to partial or total albinism, the anterior feathers were colored, not white. Carotenoid pigments, which are the basis for the pinkish-orange (or red and yellow) color, are unaffected by albinism. Thus, the red epaulet in males is unaffected and in albino females is much more prominent than usual. These masked colors of the Redwing may represent an earlier ancestral trait.

The bright-colored patches on many members of the blackbird family are often associated with displays related to courtship, fighting, or other behavioral activities. In the Redwing, for example, the red "shoulder" patches or "epaulets" (lesser wing coverts) are usually concealed by overlapping plumage, a distinction illustrated for the first time (as far as I am aware) in a painting in Roger Tory Peterson's 1980 field guide. A Redwing at rest during the nonbreeding season, or when intimidated, usually shows only the buff-colored lower edge of the epaulets (black in certain subspecies), a mark that fades to white by midsummer. The red patches, however, are conspicuous during the breeding season, and in courtship and territorial display they are prominently displayed. But even during this season, when a male trespasses on another's territory, or when males feed close together off the breed-

Bobolink

J. CARSON
1983
ⓒ

ing grounds, the red epaulets are concealed. In flight, of course, the red
wing patches are always visible. Bright vermillion is the most common color, but individuals (and subspecies) have epaulets that vary
from scarlet to orange-chrome.

The Bobolink male displays his cream-colored nape feathers while
giving a deep bow; the Western Meadowlark stands up straight to
show off his bright yellow and black breast. The male Yellow-headed
Blackbird displays his bright golden head and throat when he sings,
stretching his neck far over his left shoulder as if to show the greatest
expanse of color. It is one of the few asymmetrical displays in the
birds of this group. Even the blackest blackbirds ruffle their plumage
when displaying; the Brewer's Blackbird, at least, erecting its black
"epaulets" during song-spread (see chapter 3). Because of the dark,
matching plumage, the raised feathers are generally overlooked by observers. The Common Grackle, Brewer's Blackbird, and Rusty Blackbird have white or yellow eyes that contrast strongly with their plu-

mage. In the Common Grackle, a rapid arhythmical blinking of the nictitans, or third eyelid, has been observed by Robert Ficken as an escape reaction display.

The vocalizations of icterids are as rich and varied as their appearance, ranging from the squawk and clatter of the grackles to the clear, flutelike notes of the Northern Oriole. And the *spink, spank, spink* of "Bob o'-lincoln" (from "Robert of Lincoln" by William Cullen Bryant) is surely one of the sweetest sounds on prairie and meadow. Some icterids produce a sound by vibrations from their wings while flying. The Yellow-headed Blackbird is a good example; often, while slowly flying from one perch to another, a dull whistling sound may be heard from its wings, a sound lacking during ordinary flight.

Alexander Skutch reports:

The flight of the males of many species of the troupial family is accompanied by a characteristic sound made by the passage of the wind through the primaries. This does not depend entirely on the size and weight of the bird, for the wings of some of the smaller orioles are resonant in flight. The sound made by the Giant Cowbird as he flies is particularly loud, and of a peculiar quality suggesting that the feathers are stiff and vibrant.

The student of bird behavior finds this one of the most interesting of avian families because of the great diversity in social habits, nest construction, and modes of display associated with courtship and mating. This diversity is well evident among the North American birds. The Yellow-headed Blackbirds, Red-winged Blackbirds, and Tricolored Blackbirds are colonial, that is, they breed in close groups or colonies and mostly remain together during the nonbreeding season. Tricolored Blackbirds nest practically side by side, but they vigorously defend a small area surrounding the nest. The orioles, on the other hand, are relatively solitary in their habits. Bobolinks and meadowlarks build simple grass-lined nests right on the ground, usually in a shallow depression and concealed by a tuft of grass. Their nests are notably difficult to find. Northern Orioles build complex, woven pouches that hang from the tips of high branches.

The Brown-headed Cowbird relies on parasitizing the nests of other birds of many species. The female cowbird keeps a close and silent watch on the behavior of nesting birds and, at the appropriate moment, quietly slips in and deposits an egg in the unguarded nest. Redwings are not immune to the cowbird, though the pressure is much lighter than on some other species. Beer and Tibbitts, for example, found cowbird eggs in only six of 270 Redwing nests at Wingra Marsh, Wisconsin.

The Red-winged Blackbird is found breeding wherever there are marshes or suitable uplands from southern Alaska and northern Canada south to Costa Rica. Arthur C. Bent states:

> The numerous subspecies of the redwing are widely spread all over the continent of North America, except in the arid desert, the higher mountain ranges, the forested and the Arctic regions, wherever they can find suitable marshes in which to breed. The presence of water, or at least its proximity, is essential; and the birds must have certain types of dense vegetation in which to conceal their nests. Marshes or sloughs supporting extensive growth of cattails, bulrushes, sedges, reeds, or tules are their favorite breeding haunts; but where similar types of vegetation, or water-loving bushes or small trees, grow in ponds, around the shores of lakes or along the banks of sluggish streams, the redwings find congenial homes.

But the Redwing also nests in damp meadows and especially alfalfa fields, often a long way from water, relying on dew-sodden vegetation for nest material.

The Redwing is the most widespread of the Icteridae and is probably the most abundant bird species in North America. The total breeding population has been estimated by Patrick Weatherhead and Roger Bider as 200 million, a figure that doubles each fall with the addition of young. But the high annual mortality of young birds and lesser mortality of adults returns the figure to 200 million each year. In 1976 Brooke Meanley and Willis Royall estimated the U.S. population as 189,524,000 birds.

As a consequence of such a broad breeding range, the species comprises fourteen subspecies or geographic races, each of which has evolved slight differences, mostly in size and plumage. As yet there is little reason to think that the basic behavior of any of the subspecies differs significantly from that of the "nominate" race—*Agelaius phoeniceus phoeniceus*, the eastern race.

The Rusty Blackbird, a surprisingly little-studied bird, has a restricted range. It breeds only in the northern forests of Alaska, Canada, and New England, from the northern limits of trees southward to the edge of the boreal forest. It is the most northern of all the Icteridae, breeding within the Arctic Circle. Most of us know the Rusty Blackbird only as a migrant in spring and fall, and this is why so little is known about its habits. In 1960 I went to Uranium City in northernmost Saskatchewan to study Rusty Blackbirds. Tom Heaslip, a miner at the former Lorado uranium mine and a good amateur birder, had advised me that Rusty Blackbirds were nesting in the vicinity of the mine. I found them as he had instructed—a few widely scattered pairs nesting on the edges of ponds in a deep rock-walled valley that is so characteristic of the north shore of Lake Athabasca.

During courtship as well as incubation, I regularly saw—and with

Fred Lahrman's assistance filmed—the male feeding the female, a real benefit at this cold latitude. The Rusty Blackbird is apparently the only icterid in which courtship feeding is commonplace, though others exhibit the behavior. Courtship feeding has been reported, for example, for the Yellow-headed Blackbird, the Rusty Blackbird, the Northern Oriole, the tropical Melodious Blackbird, and the Brewer's Blackbird. But no one seems to have observed it in the Redwing. Rather, the typical Redwing behavior is for the male to ignore or even turn away from his mate. My field notes of April 16, 1952, record the following episode: "Male BRBX goes down to food on the road—and at once his female—some 60 feet away—goes there and walks up to him as he breaks off a piece of bread; he hurriedly moves aside with his piece and she feeds alone."

There ought to be some distinction between feeding by the male during the courtship period, that is, before incubation, and feeding during later stages, when the female is unable to leave the nest to search for food. This is really maintenance feeding, essential to the well-being of the female and the eggs. In the pair of Rusty Blackbirds I watched, the female would either leave the nest briefly at the male's appearance with food and then beg, or else beg while on the nest. In many species of other families, the male performs maintenance feeding, bringing all the food for the female and the young.

Many of the hardier icterids winter in the northern states and occasionally in southern Ontario, but the bulk of the "blackbirds" winter in the southern United States, roosting in great numbers (see chapter 10).

On the other hand, some icterids go far south; the orioles, for example, travel to Central America and northern South America. The familiar Bobolink makes the greatest journey of all, traveling to the pampas of Argentina. Actually, though we tend to think of these birds as "native" species, they may spend only three months of the year in North America. Thus, the Bobolink is actually more familiar with landscapes of Argentina, though breeding in meadows in the United States and Canada. This little bird (as well as other species) knows well the pattern of two continents, twice each year flying between the grasslands of southern South America and its northern breeding grounds.

It is curious that of all the icterids only the Bobolink has a double molt. By late summer the males have molted to a femalelike plumage. Before leaving the wintering ground in the pampas of Argentina, they molt again, reassuming the strongly marked black and white plumage that makes the male bird so easy to identify.

T. Gilbert Pearson was editor-in-chief of a group of prominent ornithologists and writers, including Edward H. Forbush and John Burroughs, who produced the substantial *Birds of America*, in 1917. This book, republished in 1936, includes a good description of the characteristics of the Icteridae from which the following is quoted:

In this family the bill varies greatly as to relative length and thickness, but it is never conspicuously longer than the head and always more or less conical and sharp; the outlines are usually nearly straight, but sometimes the tip curves downward. The nostrils are never concealed although sometimes the membrane immediately behind them is covered. The bristles at the corner of the mouth are altogether obsolete or but faintly developed. The wing is extremely variable (though all have nine primaries), but usually the tip is moderately extended and terminates abruptly. The tail is variable as to relative length, form of tip, and shape of the feathers; it is always more than half as long as the wing but never conspicuously longer than the wing, never forked nor notched and is usually rounded, sometimes double-rounded, and occasionally graduated and folded like a fan; usually the tail feathers, which always number twelve, are of nearly equal width throughout, but sometimes they are wider at the tips and sometimes narrower; in one species, the Bobolink, they abruptly taper to a point and are rigid at the tips.

The *Icteridae* comprise birds of most various habits. Some live among the trees, and if placed on the ground they are almost incapable of progression; others are terrestrial (though frequently alighting on trees and sometime nesting there) and walk upon the ground with the grace and dignity of a Crow. . . .

Many species are remarkable for the fullness and richness or other remarkable character of their notes, some of them being songsters of high merit, while others utter only the most harsh and discordant sounds. . . .

Icterids range in length from 6¾ to 21½ inches. A few species have a neck ruff and a few have a sparse crest. In some of the larger species the bill is rather heavy and casqued (helmetlike). Icterids generally have strong feet; the sexes are unalike in most species.

Vivid accounts of the habits of ten Central American icterids, and a general summary of the family Icteridae, have been well rendered by Alexander Skutch, who points out that profound differences in coloration between the sexes are found in the extra-tropical species and the northern icterids. The mostly nonmigratory tropical species have essentially similar plumages.

Peter E. Lowther analyzed the family Icteridae in 1975 in terms of geographic and ecological variation. Some of his conclusions are: "morphological variation within Icteridae (in the form of sexual dimorphism) may be best explained as results of 2 types of selection. Intersexual competition is the selective force behind sexual dimorphism in size and epigamic [male-female attraction] sexual selection is the cause of plumage dimorphism. . . . Plumage dimorphism is more common within the family at higher latitudes; size dimorphism more commonly occurs at lower latitudes."

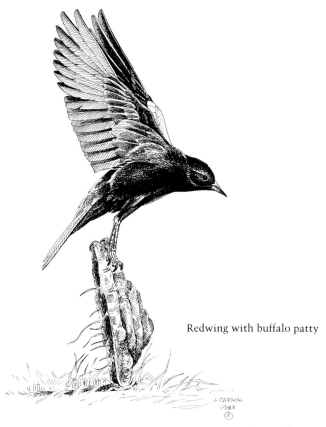

Redwing with buffalo patty

An interesting array of homologous displays and courtship and mating activities has been shown for many icterids; these behavioral affinities point to close relationships between certain species.

In his 1980 book on marsh-nesting blackbirds, Gordon Orians makes special mention of the function in Icterids of "gaping," pushing the bill into or under something to obtain prey—in cattails, bulrush, on the ground, and so forth. He notes that it is a habit found in several marsh-nesting members of the blackbird family. Skutch tells this about the Boat-tailed Grackle in Central America: "On bare shingly flats along the shores they turn over small stones by inserting the tip of the bill beneath the nearer edge and pushing forward, then devour the small crustacea, insects, worms or the like that they find beneath. It is chiefly the more powerful males that hunt in this fashion."

I saw birds at the Vilas Park Zoo in Madison, Wisconsin, regularly use their bills to tip up or push over dung in the animal pens in search of prey. One day, however, I observed one do something that astonished me: a first-year male Redwing, confronted with a large, dry buffalo or bison patty, grasped the nearer edge with his feet, flew up with it still held in his feet, and thus tipped it over! He then searched for food on the newly exposed ground. When, I wondered, did he learn that unusual technique?

2

Wingra Marsh Study Area

Physical Factors

Roughly 600 feet at its greatest length and 200 feet at its greatest
width, the marsh in which I spent six seasons lies on the southeast
corner of Lake Wingra, Wisconsin, hence my use of the name: Wingra
Marsh (officially East Wingra Marsh, a part of the University of Wisconsin Arboretum). An earthen dike, built before 1940, closes off the
small bay that forms the marsh, and affords protection to the paved
road that skirts its inner border. The dike was lined with willow, as-
pen, poplar, and cottonwood trees (as well as shrubs), which provided
good landmarks and much-used perches for Redwings holding territories on that side of the marsh.

The marsh was bordered by trees along the dike and adjacent to
the road. Within the marsh, cattail dominated; at the west end, sedge
extended to wooded upland from where I often heard Barred Owls calling. Some black willows and red osier dogwood grew along the marsh
edge by the road, providing perches for Redwings. In the central area of
the marsh there were some open areas, about three feet deep at high
water. These open sites had a hard bottom and were not invaded by

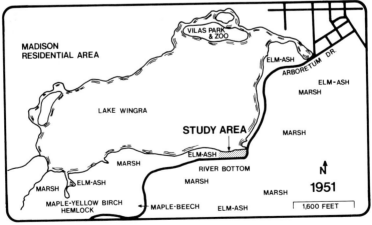

Lake Wingra, Madison, Wisconsin, showing the location of the Redwing study
area. The land south and east of Lake Wingra is part of the University of Wisconsin Arboretum.

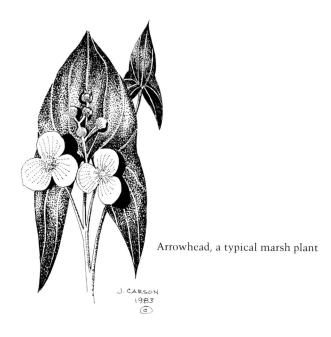

Arrowhead, a typical marsh plant

J. CARSON
1983
©

cattail. Apart from a few scattered dead trees, the marsh was otherwise open in aspect. The cattail stands, though heavily used by muskrats, remained surprisingly fixed, with numerous trails used by us and by muskrats.

Cattails usually grow in compact masses, and the growth of several years remains as dead stalks and leaves, presenting a formidable obstacle to walking. The dead material is harsh and firm. More than once I have pulled cattail slivers from my fingers. Each spring, however, new growth makes its way upward until the old beds are concealed again by green vegetation. Then the long, new cattail leaves may reach above one's head.

(In June 1982, I revisited Wingra Marsh. The road has been widened and with high water the cattails grow to its edge. There are now no trees along the dike or in the marsh.)

Park and Zoo Feeding Grounds

I think Wingra Marsh birds learned to eat bread at a local zoo. Vilas Park Zoo, about a half-mile north of the marsh across Lake Wingra, was a favorite feeding ground for my birds. Accordingly, I spent a lot of time there, trying to trap birds and getting significant observations. Many of the animals in the zoo lived and were fed in open, fenced areas; hence, many birds came there for food.

Stale bread and baked goods seemed to be staple food items for everything from peacocks to elk. Common Grackles, Redwings, cowbirds, pigeons, and crows were frequent visitors, and when not feeding in the pens could be seen walking about on picnic tables or on the ground or perched in shade trees. Even large flocks—on one occasion I saw several hundred Brown-headed Cowbirds—were occasionally seen on the broad expanse of lawn that surrounded the zoo. Speaking of the food of Common Grackles that sometimes nested in Wingra Marsh, right out in the cattails, graduate student John Snelling noted in his 1968 study in *Auk:* "Presumably much of the bread, corn chips, noodles, and peanuts found in the nestlings' gullets were obtained at the 'Vilas Park feeding ground' (picnic tables) Nero 1956 mentions."

What a difference it was to work in Vilas Park and the zoo, following birds about on the lush green lawns or crouching down in front of the animal pens to watch female Redwings expertly dodging the aggressive jabs of male Redwings when they ventured too close. At times, the grounds were filled with people, but I soon learned to ignore them in pursuit of my birds. I must have looked a proper bird-watcher.

The author walks along a trail in Wingra Marsh in spring, about 1951. (Hugh Wilmar)

It was on the lawn by the animal pens on June 8, 1949, that I first saw an adult male Redwing "anting." This is a peculiar behavior, observed in many species of birds, whereby a bird crouches on the ground and rapidly applies ants to its plumage, picking up ants and methodically placing them on the inside of the primaries. In the process of doing this the top of the head is rubbed under the primaries in the same way that a bathing bird wipes its head.

It has long been believed that birds in this way are applying formic acid—from the ants—to parts of the plumage to repel external parasites. Joel Welty, in *The Life of Birds*, notes that there are several other explanations for this behavior: the bird wipes off the ant's formic acid before eating it; ant fluids produce pleasurable effects, relieve itching, or act as medicinal tonic on the skin; ant fluids provide physical protection for the feathers. As yet, however, no explanation of anting has been generally accepted.

My observations have since led me to wonder if birds were indirectly applying formic acid to an area where feather lice may be active, namely the head area, just that portion of the plumage that is most difficult to reach and where lice often seem to gather.

My Redwings were regular park visitors, sometimes leaving the marsh in small groups to fly north to this feeding site. I speak of males; females seldom, if ever, followed this practice. One male regularly brought back bread to feed to the nestlings. Generally, during the period when fledglings were on the marsh, males were frequently seen returning from the park, carrying bread. A Redwing flying over the open lake with a piece of white bread in its bill made a conspicuous sight. My notes indicate that on July 31, 1948, nine color-banded males were seen at the zoo during half an hour (3:00 to 3:30 p.m.). There was even some indication that males flew from the marsh close to the time when bread was thrown to zoo animals. When Redwings were feeding within the pens, their color bands were easy to spot and the birds could be observed at fairly close range.

It is curious that Redwings respond so readily to the sight of white bread as food. I once dropped a piece of bread on the shoulder of a road beside a wet ditch where there were a few Redwings. Very shortly after I backed my car away, the resident male flew down to feed on the bread. This was miles from the zoo and I wouldn't think it had ever visited there. Bread also proved attractive bait to Soras, the small rails that were regular residents at Wingra Marsh. Often they entered traps set for Redwings. Consequently, I color-banded a number of Soras, and watched with delight when I saw them moving across open areas of the marsh, their colored leg bands giving away their identity. How they managed to find the bread in traps set as much as

Sora

J. CARSON
1983
©

three feet above the water on dead cattail stalks, I don't know. Most
birds lack a sense of smell. I wonder about the Sora?

Observation Methods

For my first year of study (1948), I simply stood on the edge of the
road beside the marsh trying to keep an eye mainly on one bird, but in
1949 I relied upon a wide board nailed about twelve feet up between
two trees midway along the dike as an observation point. Most of the
marsh was visible from this perch, and the three territories directly in

J. CARSON
1983
©

front of me were especially well in view. I waded through the marsh or walked along the dike, then clambered up a series of boards nailed on the side of one tree. It wasn't much of a platform, but it immediately brought me closer to the marsh. When the trees moved in the wind off the lake, so did I. Once a Common Flicker swept up to an abrupt landing on one of the support trees, right beside my face. There was a brief pause, it gave me a quick, hard look, and then it was gone, the force of its springing away moving the whole structure.

Despite the better view it provided, the board was a little awkward to stand on, and much Redwing behavior still took place out of sight, deep in the heavy cattail growth. The following year (1950) I built two observation towers twelve feet above the water, farther out in the marsh, with the aid of several fellow graduate students. These towers served thereafter as primary watch points, convenient and effective. I had to wear hip waders to get to them, but they were ever so much more comfortable and effective than the board in the trees. Now I could look down on the marsh and see practically everything, and

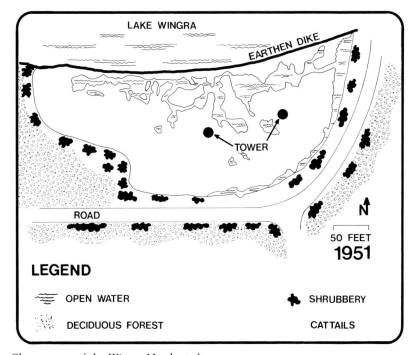

Closeup map of the Wingra Marsh study area.

The author points to a territorial male Redwing perched on a Wingra Marsh observation tower. (Hugh Wilmar)

Here the author nears the top of the observation tower. (Hugh Wilmar)

here I spent many days. Redwings soon learned to ignore me in the towers, even though I was not far above them. This was also true for ducks, which occasionally dropped into the open water in the center of the marsh; muskrats swam by unconcernedly and occasionally I watched a mink searching for prey.

Other Nesting Species

The marsh attracted several nesting species besides Redwings, including Marsh Wrens, Soras, and Virginia Rails. A nest of Least Bitterns in the midst of a heavy stand of cattails caught my attention and I made a minor study of this species (published in 1950 in *Passenger Pigeon*). Because it was the habit of the young to leave the nest at my approach, crawling off through the cattails, I fenced them in, using a circular piece of wire screen. The parents seemed not to notice it, flying in from above. By means of the fence, which rested in the water and

J. CARSON
1983
©

extended about two feet above the nest, I kept the young available at the nest site for up to sixteen days. No interaction with Redwings was observed.

I paid little attention to Common Grackles, a few of which nested in cattails along one edge of the marsh, but noted that Redwings were often antagonistic to them. James Beer reported first seeing grackles nesting in the marsh in 1946. John Wiens made a comprehensive study of interactions between grackles and Redwings at Wingra Marsh in 1962 and 1963. By that time the number of grackles had increased considerably, and several grackle nests were found right out in the cattails, sometimes in Redwing territories. Most interactions between grackles and Redwings were initiated by Redwings, whose aggressive behavior forced grackles to limit their courtship flights and visits to their nests by moving between Redwing territorial boundaries. Early flights by grackles were apparently made at random, but gradually they adjusted to the pressure of territorial male Redwings. Female Redwings showed considerable antagonism toward grackles, at least at their nest sites, but away from the nests showed little interest in them. Although rarely aggressive to Redwings, grackles dived several times at Redwings of either sex when the latter approached grackle nests too closely.

In 1965 and 1966, John Snelling undertook a detailed study of the feeding habits of Redwings and grackles nesting in Wingra Marsh. Principal Redwing foraging areas included the shrubbery in an adjacent Southern Lowland Deciduous Forest, the marsh itself, and grass around the marsh and at a large area 300 yards to the southeast. Grackles were known to scavenge at Vilas Park a half mile to the north and were believed to forage on the floor of the deciduous forest as well as around the lake edge. Animal matter, chiefly insects, predominated in the diet of both Redwings and grackles. Vegetable material occurred in only 8 percent of the samples of Redwings, while 67 percent of the grackle samples contained vegetable matter (mostly bread). However, vegetable matter in the latter diet comprised only about 19 percent of

44

Pied-billed Grebe   Hooded Merganser

the total intake by volume. Lepidoptera (mostly larvae) accounted for 64 and 18 percent of the total intake by volume of Redwings and grackles respectively. According to Snelling, competition for food was not significant beween Redwings and grackles at Wingra Marsh, but the two species were apparently competing for space.

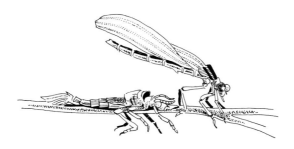

Redwing Seasonal Activities

Resident male Redwings returned to Wingra Marsh from their southern wintering grounds about the third week of March, and by late April male territories were well established. Females arrived later, former residents appearing a week or two after the males; younger females came still later. Female arrival was a period of great activity, males seeking to attract them and repel male trespassers, males in adjacent territories displaying to each other, and females dispersing throughout the marsh. There were signs of intrafemale conflict, especially between females within a given male's territory.

Egg-laying began in May and with the commencement of incuba-

The author bands a fledgling Redwing. (Hugh Wilmar)

tion, female activity was reduced. Although the marsh was the center
of activities for the Redwings, both males and females fed in adjacent
wooded areas, so there were always some birds flying in and out of the
marsh. Females and young, along with some males, left the marsh in
July, hence that month marked the beginning of breakup of the territories, though there were usually a few late-nesting birds each year.
But by the middle of August the marsh was silent.

Trapping and Banding

Eventually, I undertook to try to capture and color-band all the Redwings on the marsh that were not already banded by Beer. This in-

cluded trapping birds that had lost a color band, so that they could be identified and rebanded. In 1948, for example, Beer and Tibbitts had twenty color-banded males resident on the marsh. The aluminum government band went on either the right or the left leg, topped by a color band, plus two color bands on the opposite leg. By placing the metal band on one leg or the other, and using red, blue, green, yellow, and white color bands (celluloid coils), a large number of combinations were possible; no two birds, whether young or adult, carried exactly the same combination. By applying a drop of cement to the inside of the outermost ring of each color band, waiting a few seconds, and then compressing the band slightly, it was possible to get a band that was glued together—a more or less permanent identification mark.

Some birds carried their full complement of bands for five or six years; one bird bore some of his bands for nine years. I soon learned to identify birds by the combination of bands, using, in some cases, an X for the aluminum band and initials for the color bands. Thus, WXBR (or W/BR in my notes) had a metal band on the left leg topped with a white band, and blue over a red band on the right leg. Newly banded adult birds were seldom seen to peck at their bands, other behavioral considerations making greater demands. I felt a little reluctant to encumber nestlings with this load of bands, but, again it didn't seem to hamper them and the results of a large number of banded birds on the marsh made for an effective study. Rather than burden the reader with my color-code identification symbols for individual birds (e.g., WXRY), when I wish to describe complex situations I have usually substituted letters and numbers, such as male A, territory A, female A-1, and so on.

From 1948 through 1952, I banded 282 birds, including 175 nestlings or fledglings. Trapping Redwings for banding was a continual activity. Incidentally, for some unknown reason, dark, drizzly days were best for trapping Redwings. I used single or multiple "Potter" traps (small wire-cage, treadle-sprung bird traps) and one large walk-in trap that could accommodate several birds at once. Beer had most of these already in operation, the large walk-in trap being on top of the remains of a muskrat house. The traps were invariably placed on muskrat "push-ups" and houses, on the ground along the dike, on wire screen platforms pressed onto old standing cattail stalks, and on floating boards.

When I was trying to catch a particular individual, the trap was placed within the bird's territory, often close to a favorite perch. This was important because resident birds were reluctant to cross a neighbor's boundary. In April 1948, I set a trap for one particular male. After a few days during which the male had never approached the trap, I realized that it was set within the territory of the adjacent resident male. I immediately moved the trap a few feet and within an hour the bird was in the trap. A few trap-shy females were finally captured in an improvised trap, tripped with a string that was set on top of their nests (which held eggs or young).

The effort involved in trapping and banding Redwings was considerable; this, plus color-banding nestlings and fledglings, was extremely important to the overall study of the species. Banding unknown birds off the marsh, for example at Vilas Park, had benefits. New birds often appeared at Wingra Marsh and involvements with other birds there could be followed because they arrived already banded, carrying their identification. On a number of occasions this made all the difference in understanding what was taking place.

(In June 1982, I learned that Wingra Marsh was still being used as a training grounds for ornithologists and for Redwing studies. A student working under University of Wisconsin Professor Tim Moermond has been color-banding Redwings and marking their nests. I was thrilled to see the marsh—which seemed smaller than I remembered— and colored ribbons dangling from cattails near nests.)

Each spring I trudged throughout the marsh, slipping along the ice remaining in the several trails I had made through the cattails. Gradually, these trails deepened, though there was a high edge of ice among the adjacent cattails long after the open areas had turned to water. One had to tiptoe through the open sites ("hip boots" or "waders" are really only "crotch boots") to avoid getting wet, and one stepped up with caution to get onto the ice pan in the cattails.

When the water was high in spring, pike entered the marsh through one or more narrow gaps in the dike, coming in to spawn among the reeds. A few carp also entered the marsh and thrashed about in the emergent vegetation in their fashion. And one year a dogfish or bowfin had its spawning bed somewhere in the open area in the marsh. One morning I watched with great interest from the tower as the guarding female bowfin led her school of fingerlings across a bay. An oval rippling pattern following close behind the furrowed V that marked the progress of the adult showed where the school of small bowfins traveled. The mother fish took a short cut to an outlet, thrusting through shallow water amid the cattails, moving so far and so rapidly along a crooked pathway that I thought she would lose her offspring. But the school of young followed her exact trail, presumably guided by her scent.

Another time, a Great Blue Heron appeared high overhead, gliding toward the lake from the east. It was at a considerable height, perhaps a hundred yards. As it drew closer it suddenly side-slipped, falling a few yards, first to one side and then to the other, finally leveling out briefly. *Then* it did a surprising feat: it tipped forward until it was falling straight down, slowly *rotating* as it dropped for a considerable distance. It was an extraordinary sight. It shortly leveled out, again side-slipped to both right and left, then dropped its long legs and landed on the lake side of the dike. It was an efficient way of coming down from a height to land almost directly underneath itself. Perhaps Great Blue Herons have done this before, but I have never seen it at any other time, nor have I read about aerial skills of this merit in any book or journal.

My studies on the small Wingra Marsh enabled me to observe and describe patterns of behavior that apply throughout most of North America, wherever Redwings occur. No finer field teaching opportunity is so readily available. Even one or two male Redwings in a cattail-filled roadside ditch provide an outdoor laboratory unexcelled for observing animal behavior. Fortunately, Redwings are abundant and widespread—any school teacher should be able to find a site to demonstrate to a class the beauty and complexity of the lives of wild birds by watching Redwings.

The observation towers gave me a good view of most of the marsh and I spent many days in them. The sides of the platforms were covered with burlap to screen my movements and to allow a breeze to blow through. Observations generally were made while I stood leaning against the railing, which was at waist height. Those were glorious days, despite the few predators. Alone on the platform, surrounded by the small wilderness of the marsh and surrounding woods, learning almost daily something new about Redwings, it was pleasant enough.

My field notes don't include one incident that stands out in my memory of those days. Standing quietly on my parapet one afternoon, on a warm summer day, I spied in secrecy on a loving couple in a canoe drifting slowly in the lake adjacent to the marsh. They were in each other's arms, quite unaware that I was looking down upon them with considerable envy.

3

Some Basic Displays of Territorial Birds

Male Primary Song

Song is perhaps the most familiar form of territorial display by birds ("display" being anything that serves for communication). Anyone who has been near a marsh in spring has heard male Red-winged Blackbirds, but describing their song is another matter. I like what Arthur Allen modestly noted in 1914 in setting out to describe Redwing vocalizations: "To attempt to put in words what such men as Baird, Brewer, and Ridgway [1874] have considered indescribable, may appear somewhat rash." Allen noted further: "The greatest difficulty lies in the selection of words, letters, or symbols that will convey a sound similar to that uttered by the bird." He used *con-cur-ee, kong-quer-ree,* and *gur-gel-lee* as common renditions of the basic or primary song.

In my work with Redwings I chose *oak-a-lee* or *oak-a-ree* as most descriptive (leaving *aujourd'hui* for Canada's French-speaking bird watchers). Ardythe McMaster, a Winnipeg teacher, told me that when she was young her mother always referred to the song as *Purple-tea!* Aretas A. Saunders, musical master of bird songs, had much to say about the Redwing (in Bent's 1958 *Life Histories*). I have quoted only a portion of his notation:

The song of the redwing, well known to bird lovers as *conqueree*, is actually much more variable than this simple rendition. It generally consists of from 1 to 6 short notes, followed by a somewhat longer trill. The quality is pleasing, and the presence of prominent liquid and explosive consonant sounds gives it a gurgling sound.
The *conqueree* song, to my ear more like *ko-klareeee*, is by far the commonest form, the first note being lowest in pitch, the second medium, and the trill highest. . . .
A peculiar variation, of which I have 9 records, has the trill made up of notes slow enough to be heard separately and counted. In such cases the number of notes in the trill varies from 5 to 7. Such songs usually have but 1 note before the trill, so that such a song sounds like *ka-lilililip.*

Once, I found a group of territorial males singing in just that fashion at Mud Lake, not far from Madison, Wisconsin. I recorded the distinctive call of this small group of males as *"oak-a-le he he he."*

All observers agree that Redwing primary song (the basic territorial vocalization), despite variations from one locality to another, occurs in three parts—introductory notes and a terminal trill. The song, as with nearly all vocalizations, is highly variable, depending on motivation. It varies in intensity, pitch, and duration, but can easily be recognized as the basic or primary song of the male of this species.

A highly technical study of primary song by Douglas G. Smith et al. (1980) concludes that "The Red-winged Blackbird 'conc-a-ree' song consists of two basic components: a variable number of rather stereotyped introductory notes followed by a trill that varies in duration both within and between renditions. . . . Each male retains some variability by being able to select one rendition or another while also showing stereotype for each delivery."

Orians and Christman tape-recorded all known vocalizations of male Redwings, presenting graphic sonograms of primary song and eleven other vocal utterances that provide a more direct means of comparison. They note that at Jewel Lake, California, male Redwings "gave an average of 172 songs per hour while on their territories and observations elsewhere suggest that this is typical." Working at Wingra Marsh, Beer and Tibbitts found males singing in late April at a peak about 540 songs per hour (90 in ten minutes), or nine each per minute, from 8:00 to 8:10 a.m. That's almost continuous song and it would certainly decrease over an average daily period.

There is a general tendency toward geographical differences in dialect among birds of a given species over wider geographical areas than I describe here. It is a phenomenon well known to ornithologists. I knew a marsh about twenty miles from my study area where most males sang "oak-a-lee-ink!" It was a local dialect, and once only, a bird with this song type appeared at Wingra Marsh, sang with the "ink" ending, and departed. I was sure it was from that other marsh.

Redwing studies advanced again when Eliot A. Brenowitz undertook a detailed analysis of song, playing back parts to determine more precisely the significance of the vocalizations. He found that although there was considerable variation in the introductory notes, the trill is given in fairly standard fashion. Other recent studies indicate increased complexity in type of primary song and function. For example, males have been shown to have as many as eight distinct types of song, which they tend to synchronize with changes of perch, and they sing many renditions of a single song type before switching to another. It has also been shown that song functions primarily in territory defense, but some experimentally muted males were still able to maintain their territories.

Elaborate studies of male primary song involving playback experiments with altered tape recordings showed that only the trill portion of the song elicited aggressive response and that the trill functions in species recognition. Douglas Smith reported in 1979 that after he had temporarily muted territorial males by means of a simple operation (the effect lasting two to three weeks), intrusions by their neighbors were more frequent and the treated birds resorted to increased visual display (sidling in an aggressive manner). After the treated birds regained full vocalization, however, they quickly reestablished their original boundaries.

Song-spread Display

On the breeding grounds, primary song is usually accompanied by a display of plumage, particularly spreading of the wings and tail. The combined display (hence my use of the term "song-spread") provides further measure of its emphasis, the motivation, and, to some extent, the function. The behavior of a bird giving song-spread typically involves spreading the wings and tail out fully, thrusting the head forward and upward. All the body plumage is raised. At the onset of song, the spread tail is brought down, the wings expand to maximum spread, and, in extreme display, the red epaulet feathers or wing coverts are raised. It is a stunning effect.

There is, as I said, a considerable range of degree of display, depending on the motivation. On a cold March morning with only one or two males in sight, we're lucky to get even a little raising of plumage and a feeble song—a great contrast with the flashing of plumage and extended terminal phrase *"leee!"* heard repeatedly across the marsh when females are first arriving and males seemingly strive to outdo each other in presenting themselves. Song-spread display appears to function primarily in territorial defense, but it also has been shown to influence female recruitment. I believe song-spread is most extensive when directed toward a particular male. Ken Yasukawa in Indiana, using a male dummy, a tape recorder, and a microphone, made a quantitative analysis of Redwing song-spread and aggressive tendencies. He concluded: "Song-spread intensity can be interpreted as an indication of the aggressive tendencies of male redwings in situations where actual attack is inhibited. . . .threat display and other behavior have signal value and indicate to an intruder the possibility of attack."

While song-spread may be given more frequently and extensively in the presence of females, it appears to be directed mainly to other males. A resident male involved in courting a female, crawling through the cattails, will occasionally stop, climb up and deliver a rousing song-spread to his neighbors, then drop down and resume his quiet, out-of-sight courtship activity. Also, song-spread is given long before there are any females on the marsh. Male flocks in spring and fall are frequently in nearly continuous song (though without the spreading of plumage), producing a chorus not without musical merit, though generally clamorous.

Curiously, on one occasion I observed adult males giving full song-spread in two breeding sites at midday late in the season. The date was November 1, 1952; one place was on the Madison campus at the "University Bay" marsh on Lake Mendota. Five or six adult males behaved as if they were on territory, giving song-spread many times with *raised epaulets.* They may have been summer residents returned to territories, but they were not banded birds. I saw two isolated birds climb up on separate stalks; first one, then the other gave song-spread. Several times birds gave the territorial flight-song (see page 57) recorded in my field notes on this occasion as *"seee-tcheek-tcheek-tcheek."* My notes say: "It looked and sounded like Spring." Later that day I heard several others singing at Mud Lake. Another observer, Maurice L. Giltz, wrote to me recently: "On bright sunny autumnal days in October and early November birds set up territories similar to those in the spring. Several times marked birds were found there on their former nesting territories." This was in upland habitat in Ohio.

Orians discovered autumnal breeding in the Tricolored Blackbird in sunny California, but I know of no indication that Redwings have ever been recorded breeding in the fall. Many songbirds show a slight increase in male hormone in autumn and I suppose that was the basis for Redwings behaving as if on territory in October and November. Robert Payne noted that in central California, resident adult Redwings began to sing in early September, but no territories were defended.

Cheryl Harding and Brian Follett have reported that in Redwings certain behavior releases hormones. Hence, the endocrine system may play an important role in adjusting an animal's minute to minute behavioral responses. Experimental treatment of captive male Redwings indicated that male hormone levels had a strong effect on dominance. William Searcy and John Wingfield presumed that this affected the success of individual males in intrasexual competition for territories and mates. Some of my photos of extreme song-spread were taken of a male responding to a male dummy placed in his territory. There was no mistaking the intent in that case: the male outdid himself repeatedly in the face of this silent, trespassing intruder.

In my opinion, it is safe to assume that birds are subject to a range of response, and the response to a particular situation is determined by a combination of experience, built-in reflexes, and feeling. In

Male song-spread display. The bird at left is displaying in response to a mounted adult male in his territory; note the raised feathers of the displaying bird in the next photo. Third from left: a male displays from his perch on a dock plant. Two cattail stalks are grasped by the displaying male third from right; the bird second from right is displaying by the dawn's early light; and, at far right, an extreme song-spread display is seen from below.

short, confronted by the image of an unmoving opponent, my male was angry. In other experimental situations I have repeatedly watched males respond to a dummy with a series of displays of increasing intensity followed by attack, which on occasion ripped the dummy open. Presumably, male hormone levels were high in these cases, but I see this as one more factor in the motivation and operation of behavior. On the other hand, on some occasions males were unresponsive to dummies.

Female Song and Song-spread Display

The female Redwing is one of the very few female songbirds that sing—yet few previous observers made note of this interesting and conspicuous phenomenon. When I published my thesis in 1956, A.C. Bent's "Life History" series on blackbirds had not yet appeared. I was

rightly embarrassed then to discover that, as pointed out in Bent, I had overlooked an early observer who, in fact, did report on female song-spread in the Redwing. This present book gives me an opportunity to redress that error.

In 1897 Thomas Proctor published an account in *Auk* (the oldest ornithological journal in North America) titled: "An Unusual Song of the Red-winged Blackbird." He wrote:

And very amusing indeed it was to watch these comedians in sober brown, but in extemporized ruffs, puffs and puckers, pirouette, bow and posture, and thus quite out-do in airs and graces their black-coated gallants. Their shrill whistle, the meantime continually vied with, or replied to, the hoarse challenges of their admirers, while in noisy chattering, and in teasing notes, they were excessively voluble.

Oddly, Bent misinterpreted this delightful description of the female song-spread performance, for later he gives an account of female song

Female song-spread display. One of the very few female songbirds that sing, the female Redwing is nearly identical in display of plumage to the male—though the song itself differs. In these views, the bird at left is giving a display of moderate intensity; third from left is a high-intensity display, rear view; and at far right is another high-intensity display.

reported by a second observer—Alexander D. DuBois—then adds, "I can find no other mention of a female song." According to DuBois: "On April 28 and 29, 1930, I heard a thrush-like song suggestive of the veery coming from somewhere beyond a house; and on May 2, I definitely saw a female red-wing singing this song at the edge of a marsh by the road."

While the song of the female differs from that of the male, the display of plumage is nearly identical. As in the male, the degree of posturing changes with the intensity of the display—from song alone to fully expanded wings and tail. Female song-spread is even more clearly directed to females. Residents watch birds passing overhead or trying to land in the marsh and display to them as furiously as described by Proctor. In extreme song-spread display even the epaulets may be raised. This is interesting since in older females there is a tendency for an increased amount of red color in those feathers; when the red-tinged epaulets of an older female are raised in song-spread there is no mistaking the homologous function of the display.

The song itself? Well, it's not a version of *"oak-a-lee"* or anything close to the male rendition. Female song consists rather of a series of chattering, scolding tones rendered in my earliest field notes as *"spit-a-chew-chew-chew."* Beginning with a short rasping sound, the female song then goes off into a series of high, shrill, and rapid notes, slowing and descending at the end. Don't, for heaven's sake, read *"spit-a-chew-chew"*; instead, purse your lips and give a short chirping sound, staccato. It's the best I can do.

Orians and Christman show sonograms of female song, calling it "female chatter" and identifying it only as "harsh and rasping." I find it not unpleasant; there are times when female song is a vibrant sound in the marsh, at times eclipsing male song. A chorus of female Redwings is one of the happiest sounds on a marsh, notes of cheer—though their song-spread display may be latent with aggression, fury, and go-away meaning.

The intensity of sound and activity on a Redwing marsh is highest early in the morning: some females are carrying strips of wet cattails for nest building, others are perched on the highest cattail stalks, "bowing and posturing" and giving shrill chattering calls. Meanwhile, the males are singing at full volume, flying slowly from point to point along their territorial boundaries, facing each other in ritualized duels—a frenzy of birdlife—not to mention calls of other marsh birds: rails, Soras, coots, and Pied-billed Grebes. There is really nothing quite like a marsh in full bloom with birdlife on a sunny morning in May.

A more halting and labored version of female song, rendered *"pee-chee-ta-chee-ta-che-ta,"* often leads into the usual call, and seems to indicate general excitement, scolding, or alarm. Female Redwings flying over a marsh may find these calls of their congeners attractive and stimulating. Redwings are, after all, colonial, and it seems likely that the very sounds that one could imagine as antagonistic are, in fact, strongly alluring.

Female Redwing song was examined in detail by Thomas Dickinson, who reported three main types at the 1981 annual meeting of the American Ornithologists' Union at Edmonton, Alberta. They were: (1) associated with the mate; (2) while encountering a female rival; and (3) while leaving a nest site. "Most commonly, these vocal complexes follow the male's song as a duet." As I sat in the audience listening to these revelations I couldn't help but wonder how I could have overlooked something so obvious. Even Proctor, as mentioned earlier, noted in 1897 that female song "continually vied with, *or replied to,* the hoarse challenges of their admirers" (italics mine).

Male Flight-song

"Flight-song" is a male display. Although it is given less frequently than song-spread, it is a means of distinguishing territorial birds. The full call, always given in flight, consists of a long, rapid series of notes something like *"tseee...tch-tch-tch-tch...cheg-chee-chee-chee,"* the middle phrase, often nasal in tone, sometimes rendered as *"tank."* Sometimes only a portion of the call is given, and often the number of notes in each phrase varies, but the call is distinctive. What is apparently the same display is mentioned by Arthur Allen in his 1914 study: "a sort of scolding song, which is given in the air, with quivering wings, can easily be resolved into: *check-check-check t'tsheah."*

Beer and Tibbitts describe a "victory display or flight song . . . normally given after successfully chasing a trespassing male from the territory." Orians and Christman identify a long complicated male song as the "Flight Call Complex," adding, "The total call may last up to 6 seconds making it the longest vocalization of the species." I quite agree with them that it is "uttered only when leaving and returning to the territory."

A rapid call that resembles the middle phrase of the flight-song (*tch-tch-tch*) is frequently given during sexual chasing, where it appears to be a scolding or threatening vocalization. One day a male repeatedly gave this call while aggressively chasing an Eastern Kingbird.

A male Redwing gives a sexual "crouch" display to a female on his territory.

Sexual Displays

"Crouching" is an indication of sexual excitement in the male. It is given mainly to specific females. From an upright position the male suddenly leans forward in a tense posture, rump feathers raised, tail down and spread, wings out and epaulets flared; often the head is withdrawn and the bill points downward. The crouch posture is assumed when the male is near one of his females, usually facing her, and often precedes further sexual activity. It is also given before new females and can be elicited by a female dummy. There is no female counterpart for this display.

Increased sexual excitement in the male is shown by a tendency to hold the wings out laterally from the body, often with raised epaulets, while uttering a soft, whimpering *"ti-ti-ti-ti,"* the sexual call. It often precedes copulation.

At Wingra Marsh sexual displays were given on several occasions to other males early in the season before any females had arrived. On March 6, 1951, an adult male at least three years old repeatedly held his wings outspread and quivering while giving the *"ti-ti"* call. This display was given alternately with full song-spread and erect epaulets to approaching flocks of male Redwings, as well as to approaching individuals, including one first-year male. From March 12 to 27, 1952, several different males were observed giving this display to other males. It seemed especially to be directed by residents toward new males, which often came in without song and with epaulets more or less concealed. These observations suggest that responses in the male that are normally geared to the female may be set off momentarily by movements or postures in other males that in part resemble or are suggestive of female characteristics. However, this does not imply an outright failure of sex-recognition.

Bill-tilting

"Bill-tilting" is a common display used in aggressive encounters by both male and female. In this display the neck is stretched upward, the bill is tilted up, and body plumage is generally compressed. It is given without sound. Males commonly use this display when confronting each other on territorial boundaries, both birds often mutually bill-tilting to each other. On one occasion, when two males were tilting to each other in a tree, the uppermost bird moved down along a branch and even hung down to display to the lower bird as the latter moved up. In antagonistic situations, bill-tilting precedes attack. Although the epaulets are visible during bill-tilting, they are not raised.

Male bill-tilting is a display commonly given by males to each other, particularly when confronting each other on territorial boundaries. Note the tightly compressed head and neck plumage of the extreme bill-tilting threat display of the bird at right.

Female bill-tilting is a display given regularly to other females (and quite often to first-year males, but rarely to adult males). The bird at right, with a fist full of reeds, is bill-tilting to another female on the same male territory.

Females regularly bill-tilt to other females, pointing up to birds passing overhead or bill-tilting to each other in the proximity of their nests. Females also bill-tilt to first-year males, but rarely to adult males. Juvenile birds use it mainly against first-year males. It is a common display in several icterids.

Male Plumage

It needs to be pointed out that males in their second summer, that is, first-year males, can be identified by their plumage. The colored wing patches of the younger birds are orange or orange-red in color, mottled with black. These birds, which frequently visit the marsh, are vigorously routed by territorial adults. Usually, they don't breed in their second summer, but I once found two on territory several miles from Wingra Marsh. They keep *trying*—there were usually a few trying to slip into the marsh, but females and males alike raise such a hue and cry that they seldom linger long. Since first-year females do breed, there is an imbalanced sex ratio in favor of females, and hence the polygynous nature of the adult male-female relationship (see chapter 5). The first-year males, as we called them, seemed to simply wander about for most of the summer, joining male flocks in fall, now in full color, prepared to breed the following or third summer.

In a paper delivered at the 1981 American Ornithologists' Union meeting, Hamilton Greenwood reported that he had examined the plumage of 1,500 subadult males. He found a great deal of variation in their color and pattern, "from perfect adult male mimics to near perfect female mimics. . . . the adult male-like plumage may be a positive adaptation to breeding as a subadult in habitats or geographical areas of reduced competition, whereas the female-like plumage may result in breeding via cuckoldry of territorial males." I think that this latter point underrates the ability of Redwings to make identifications based on overall behavior as well as appearance. Females are quick to drive away immature males and females. I think it unlikely that a young male in femalelike plumage would be able to copulate successfully with a resident female.

Adult Male Epaulets

One day, at the suggestion of Professor Nicholas Collias, I trapped one of my color-banded males and painted his scarlet feathers black with India ink. He disappeared for a day, as I thought he might, but a day later he reappeared, his epaulets looking almost normal. He sat low to the ground on the tree-lined edge of his territory and spent almost all of his time washing and scrubbing his epaulets. Now, that simple experiment didn't teach us much about the territorial significance of red epaulets, but it did say a lot about the way in which a male regarded this soiling of his bright plumage!

Much the same thing happened initially when Douglas Smith tried blacking out epaulets on territorial males. He partly clipped the red feathers, then painted the remainder with black enamel. After a week the male came back with the black enamel preened off! Within two days he had ousted two new males that had moved in and divided his vacant territory between themselves. Later, Smith used a black dye which the birds could not wash out, no matter how hard they tried. "Of the black-epauleted males more than half lost their territories to intruding males," Smith reported. "In contrast, less than 10 percent of the controls [which had their epaulets daubed with alcohol] lost their territories. This suggests that the epaulets contribute significantly to the communication of threat between rival males. Without the threatening effect of the epaulets, the black-epauleted males were at a disadvantage in maintaining their territories." Nevertheless, males with epaulets blackened prior to pair formation were able to pair and mate successfully.

Lynn Morris found that territorial males whose epaulets had been experimentally blackened in the prebreeding period were able to maintain their territories; they brought off broods successfully, but suffered more intrusion by normal adult males, which delayed the courtship sequence. During the postbreeding period, some epaulet-blackened males were displaced by normal adult males.

A Ph.D. thesis by Frank Peek was largely concerned with experimental muting and epaulet blackening of several territorial Redwings. The results of this experimental study, Peek wrote in 1972, "suggest that both vocalization and red epaulet color are essential for normal territory maintenance . . . during the first portion of the breeding season. During the remainder of the breeding season these were not essential for apparently normal territory maintenance."

On May 23,1953, I found a lone territorial male outside of Madison in submarginal habitat. There was an alarmed female present that I assumed was nesting and paired with this male, which was practically mute. Whenever this adult male gave song-spread it did so with its plumage fully spread, but it never gave more than a weak screech. At times it opened its beak as if to call—but no sound was emitted.

There are two possible explanations for the males with blackened epaulets strenuously preening and washing their discolored plumage. It may simply have been in response to the feel of disarranged plumage; the alternative is that the birds were cognizant of the change in color, were disturbed by it, and were trying to regain their normal red feathers. This is an aspect I think is largely overlooked in these experiments.

At the October 1981 meeting of the Raptor Research Foundation in Montreal, Fran Hamerstrom briefly described how she replaced worn tail feathers in a submissive and harassed immature Red-tailed Hawk, imping (cutting the old feathers off at the base and fastening on the cut ends of the new feathers) on a set of adult plumes. The result was this hawk's instant assumption of a dominant role over its two immature female penmates. It acted as if it were aware of its new, brightly colored tail. Similarly, male Redwings may have a significant awareness of their red epaulets.

A strong, positive relationship between overall size and dominance exists in male Redwings, according to a study published by William Searcy in 1980. The latter states that Redwing epaulet size and color do not seem to function as signals of dominance in adult Redwings, but the lesser degree of color in first-year males may serve to reduce adult aggression. This seems contradictory. I would suggest that adults are less aggressive toward first-year males because the latter are more readily evicted.

Drive, emotion, and motivation may be subjective terms, but I remain convinced that Redwings are finely tuned to their surroundings and that such words help explain bird behavior. The fact that old, established Redwing males recognize their neighbors, know their mates and their neighbor's mates, and show immediate change in behavior when a challenging male appears, suggests that these birds are sensitive to fine degrees of differences in appearance and behavior, and are capable of making instant responses to new situations.

4

Male Territorial Behavior

The territory of a bird seems an easy thing to understand and describe, but it is more complicated than it first appears. The territory of an adult male Redwing can be defined as the area in which it spends much of its time during the breeding season. OK, so far. But the bird is not always there. It leaves its territory for a number of reasons: to search for food, to pursue a challenging male, to chase or drive off other species.

In southern Wisconsin, adult males arrive in mid-March. Local residents, that is, birds which have previously held territories, usually arrive first. At that time of year the marsh is often deep with snow and Redwings must seek food elsewhere. The first arrival of a territorial bird is a momentous event; it has flown many hundred miles and many days to reach the marsh. In the early morning it sits on a high perch, utters soft call notes ("chk" being common, given with a slight flick of its tail), and now and then presents a weak version of its song. It may do little more than perch, sing, look around, stay a while, and then depart for one to several days, depending on the weather. It sings less often if it is alone on the marsh; more often if a few others are around. When it departs it may seek barnyards, manure scattered over snow-covered fields, and other feeding sites.

For the next several days the marsh may be cold and still. Where are the territories? When the experienced resident arrives, he knows where the heart of the territory lies; at a glance he surveys the habitat he will later claim. How claim? Watch a single male in early April when the weather is more suited for this business. He stays on a perch, often a specific branch on a tree, or the top of a willow bush. From that fixed point, the main perch, he flies out to various points in the marsh, perching on the cattails, now here, now there, but often returning to his tree (see diagram). Given the presence of other males on their territories, he is more active, flying out to make a point, to establish his claim, and in so doing, defining the boundaries of his territory. At each point he gives his song, displaying himself (or his plumage) in an ancient pattern characteristic of the species. He may spend several minutes at outlying points of his territory, especially if a neighboring male flies out to perch nearby. Thus, gradually, the territory of the bird begins to manifest itself.

Enclose all the points where the bird has perched: main tree, edge of

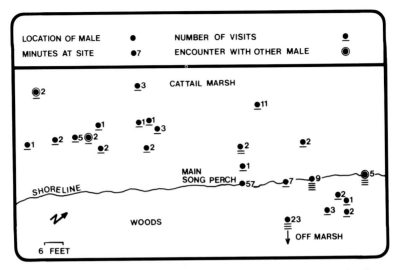

This diagram depicts the activities of one adult male at Wingra Marsh—the time spent on his main song perch and on flights to other points within his territory—from 7 to 9:30 a.m. on March 30, 1948.

woods behind the marsh, each place in the cattails (where females will eventually build their nests). This is not the territory; this is merely a summary of the movements of a territorial bird at that particular time of the year. Keep watching the bird. Other males arrive, perching on other trees, making their presence known at certain points.

As the season advances, more birds arrive until the marsh bears its usual complement of adult males. For Wingra Marsh this varied yearly, from seven to fourteen males successfully holding territories (from 1948 to 1953). With increased numbers of resident males, all returning to occupy essentially the same areas, the pressure increases. Where one bird has previously overstepped itself, perching far out into the cattails, it may now retreat, staying within a smaller area. If all the males present are previous occupants of the marsh there will be little pushing and shoving, each bird pretty well remaining within the boundaries evident the previous year. Territories are contiguous—we speak of "mutual boundaries"—and well fixed. But the death of one or more birds means some portions of the marsh are unoccupied. Then, neighbors may increase their territories, taking advantage of the new space.

Additional Territory-seeking Males

Throughout the breeding season one sees unsettled males lurking about. This floating part of the population (a characteristic of numerous species of birds) will insure that, for the most part, no suitable part of the breeding habitat goes unused. Orians, working with Redwings in California, found that when residents were experimentally removed by shooting, their territories were quickly occupied by new birds, though the rate of replacement slowed as the season advanced. Frank Peek, in Pennsylvania, found that "the surplus population of males which was present on the marsh prior to the occurrence of mating disappeared after mating." Experience gained by those birds in attempting to establish territories is considered a prime factor in successful occupancy of a territory in the following year. Such experience could be obtained by visiting territories, or occupying territories, late in the season. This would explain the attempted territoriality of nonbreeding yearling males.

One year at Wingra Marsh a resident male entered a trap within his territory some time during the day. When I arrived at the marsh in late afternoon I was surprised to find three new males fighting over the territory. As an experiment, I took the trapped bird home with me and held him overnight. Upon my arrival in the morning three birds were still present, quarreling constantly but holding ground. Within half an hour of the release of the original occupant, however, all three contenders had been driven off, and the color-banded bird was back on his perch!

Territory Boundaries—and Some Case Histories

Long-time residents know their own boundaries and respect the boundaries of their neighbors, hence there is little actual fighting over territorial rights. In Redwings the boundary lines are finely drawn, following natural vegetative outlines at times, but more often cutting across habitats to include, for example, a good tree perch. At Wingra Marsh some males even included a tree perch on the opposite side of the adjacent road. In a small cattail marsh in New Jersey, Ernst Mayr found all of six resident males using trees outside the marsh for "singing posts." It's important to be able to perch up above the tops of the cattails. A branch stuck upright in the cattails within a territory was usually quickly accepted as a perch, particularly when there were no other places to perch.

Males on territories in a cattail-filled drainage ditch (a former creek) in an industrial section of Winnipeg in May 1982 sang from the tops of vertical exhaust pipes on diesel trucks parked in a row facing the ditch. They also regularly used lamp standards along the street side of the ditch.

I don't wish to give the impression that there was no quarrel over boundaries. Occasionally, fierce battles raged between adjacent or competing males, usually at a particular place. At times, combatants rolled about in the mud and water and then rose up into the air like chickens fighting. In one instance, at another marsh, I observed such a sustained struggle between two adjacent territorial males. The battle must have gone on for some time, for birds of several species were gathered at the spot. This was on June 6, 1953. The combatants fought vigorously, practically up to their necks in water. The loser emerged with a large, easily visible blob of blood on each side of his head. He flew up into a tree and shook the blood and water from himself while the victor gave song-spread from nearby cattails. A moment later the loser flew down to his territory, adjacent to the other's and gave a large song-spread there.

A large number of birds trapped off the marsh (or newcomers to the marsh) in late May and June had partially bare scalps, undoubtedly the result of such strife. Oddly, the bare scalp of such birds was tanned or pigmented, almost black, so that the scalp, normally flesh-colored, was not readily apparent at a distance. Generally, however, Wingra Marsh males met each other with mutual song-spread and occasional bill-tilting. These frequent ritualized displays served their purpose, saving energy that would have been lost in actual combat.

Males sometimes flew to their boundaries when their mates strayed over the line; an errant female would then be brought home from the adjacent territory by a fast, direct attack from her mate, an in-and-out-again flight that left little opportunity for the territory owner to retaliate. Old resident birds were fairly tolerant of each other. For example, one spring when I tossed a piece of bread for a male onto the ice just over the boundary into another male's territory, the first male flew down quietly and fed (with red epaulets concealed!) while the owner of the territory looked on with no response.

On the other hand, there were some situations involving two or more birds and struggles that went on for many days. Let me cite one example. For a month in early spring 1952, the owner of a well-established territory, A, held a challenging male, B, 400 feet back in the woods, far from the territory (see diagram, p. 68). Whenever B made the least approach to the marsh, male A would at once launch an attack. Male A even neglected his territory to confront male B. A week later, when male A became involved in a quarrel with an even more aggressive challenger, male C, male B moved up to the edge of territory A but male B always withdrew when A took time to threaten him. Things changed drastically when male A was trapped. In the absence of any threat, male B moved in and took over the territory. Male

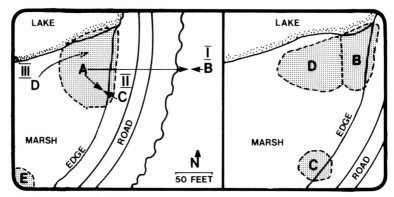

This is a case in which a resident male (A) held a challenging male (B) far off the territory. A third male (C) became involved, but later moved to another spot. When male A was trapped, his territory was divided between males D and B (right).

D, however, had also managed to slip in (he had occupied this area the previous year). Male C wound up in another contest three territories south. For a time territory A was split between the last two opponents, becoming territory D and B (see diagram). My field notes on the day of the takeover by male B follow:

April 21; 8:30 a.m.—Male A found in trap on his territory. Male B on territory in fine spirits, *doesn't move out when I go in*. Male A was badly scalped from trying to get out of the trap; this puts him at a severe disadvantage. I released him in the woods to the east where B had been. Male A was approached by B, but B did not give chase or threat. A flew farther into the woods and B returned to the marsh territory. At 5:25 p.m. I saw male A appear in the woods; at once male B flew toward him and A escaped to the east, farther into the woods. Male B stayed there singing to male A.

Male B still occupied the territory on April 24, but a few days later male A returned and in my absence reoccupied his territory.

These were the sorts of complicated situations that I was trying to observe and document for the entire marsh, year after year. A lot of information in my field notes never got into my theses! But these were exciting days and I was seeing things I never expected. Even the old adage about a male being dominant in his territory was dispelled one day when a six-year resident was completely dominated and forced off his territory by a new rival. The intruding male drove off the resident with a fierce attack, usurping the owner's favorite perch, and singing loudly. It went on in this fashion all day and the resident was not in sight the next morning. However, I found the situation reversed when I went back to the marsh that evening. What I assumed to be the invading male (unbanded) was in a trap over which the resident bird was giving jubilant song-spread display. The resident held the territory that year and the next.

In another case, a resident male (BRBX) was gradually forced off his territory by an unbanded adult male. My notes for April 23, 1952 read as follows:

5:15 p.m.—BRBX makes a pass at the unbanded male. The latter seems more excited and gives greater display than the resident. There is a lot of bill-tilting between the two, especially by the owner of the territory when the intruder approaches. But they both tilt and walk up on the main perch. BR does not display as fully as the rival. BR displays mostly when in flight when he glides over his territory. The new male gets above BR on the perch and sings down to him.

5:30 p.m.—The contest goes on and on, the new male constantly driving BR who seems to move farther east towards or onto YRWX territory, latter male remains aloof and across the road. The two rivals go up into the air in a real fight; again and again.

April 24, 4:00 p.m.—BR and the unbanded male are still on the territory and apparently still engaged in a duel. BR seems to have moved northeast of his original territory, as if squeezed out by the intruder. YWBX holds his territory as usual.

5:00 p.m.—BRBX is being threatened by the intruder who actually attacks him on his territory. Follows him about, crouches above him, flies above him in flight, drives him constantly, in short, completely dominates him so that BR is forced to sing while in flight over his own territory much as an intruder might. The new male attacks him constantly wherever he goes. A real battle takes place in the cattails; BR is always the loser. Female XYBG is present on this territory as a new resident. Perhaps she came with the unbanded intruder(?). BR chases at this female, then drives at the unbanded male who in turn chases him lower.

5:15 p.m.—BRBX sings unmolested for twenty minutes from his new song-perch about seventy feet to the east—even while the unbanded male is absent . . . he sits there all this while.

And so the contest ended.

Territory is a part of a breeding grounds, assuming active character when occupied by an adult male. Territory form responds to outside pressures, as well as to the drive or strength of the occupant. John Emlen once suggested that we think of "territorial behavior" rather than "territory." And he viewed territorial behavior as a form of social behavior in which positive and negative spacing forces are acting simultaneously.

One can talk about an unoccupied territory, but in that sense one really means a portion of a breeding grounds formerly occupied. One can observe the behavior of the resident, record his activities and those of adjacent birds, and thus, in part determine the size and shape of a territory. Wingra Marsh territories were about sixty feet square,

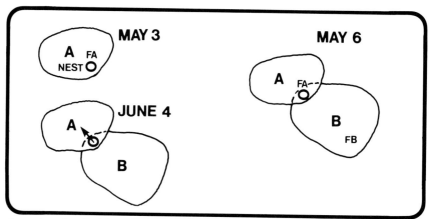

A portion of male A's territory, including an active nest, was seized by an adjacent newly arrived male (B), who was courting a second female (FB). A simple experiment (see text) showed that the first female (FA) had changed her allegiance to the new male (B). She also had a second brood with male B.

the actual shape varying with the nature of the vegetation and often including a strip that embraced a tree along the margin of the marsh. One way to determine the area held by a resident male is to walk into his territory, trying to make him fly away. Well-established birds are not easily moved outside the boundaries of their territories.

The flexibility of territory may be illustrated by one case history. In this instance a newly arrived male seized a portion of a resident's territory in which a female had already built a nest. The female stayed with her nest and later mated with the second male for a second brood. It was not clear which male she mated with for the first clutch. Male A arrived on March 28, 1952, and quickly occupied essentially the same area he had held as a territory in 1951. On April 16, female A appeared on male A's territory. She had been resident in 1951 on an adjacent territory with another male. This female associated with male A for at least the next eighteen days—until May 3 (see diagram). No observations were made on May 4 or 5, but on May 6 a newly arrived male, B, in adult plumage for the first time (second-year male), was observed holding a portion of male A's territory that included female A's completed nest. Male B was also courting a new female (FB). On this day male A still showed an attachment to female A, but also a respect for the new male. On May 20 and 28, male A still showed an interest in and a tolerance of female A, but on June 3, when she was feeding fledged young, he seemed antagonistic toward her.

Since it was not clear whether male and female A were entirely separated, a simple experiment was performed on June 4 which showed this to be the case. Two caged young of female A's brood were placed well within territory A; for half an hour male A kept female A from feeding her young. Female A later nested again but with male B. In this case it appeared that the territorial claim made by male B caused female A to relinquish the social bond originally established between herself and male A. An extraordinary situation! The field observer is well advised to watch for situations, such as the above, that deviate from the norm, for in this way the dynamic nature of basic behavior patterns may be revealed.

Generally, when females move across territory boundaries to renest they necessarily mate with new males. In one case, however, a female remained with her mate even though she nested on an adjacent territory. In May 1950, a female (FA) deserted a completed nest for unknown reasons and renested successfully in an adjacent territory belonging to male B, though retaining her original mate (A). Her encroachment on B's territory was not observed by me but on at least one occasion I saw him chase her. Occasionally, the female was joined by her mate (A); apparently the tolerance shown by the resident male (B) to the intruding female was partly extended to the latter's mate. Results obtained from experimentally moving a fledgling showed, however, that the original territory boundary had not shifted and was recognized by both males. Hence the nest in question was actually located on a foreign territory. (See diagram illustrating boundary relationships, p. 72.)

Margaret Nice describes in detail how a female Song Sparrow, which built her fourth nest on a neighbor's territory, fought with the male owner and finally dominated him. Her mate later also fought the male and by that means procured the area of her nest as part of his territory.

In the case I described above, although male A was occasionally tolerated within B's territory, he did not claim any of the latter's territory. In the succeeding year, the female left male A and bred on B's old territory with a new male, which had succeeded in ousting male B. Let's not call her a fickle female. Let's say instead that she found the habitat in B's territory more to her liking than the habitat in A's territory.

In a similar case in the Snow Bunting, Niko Tinbergen tells how a female built a nest outside of her mate's territory. After a few days the male joined her, attacked the original owner, and after two days' fighting, seized the area in the vicinity of the nest.

Len Howard tells how one pair of Great Tits, occupying a nest-box

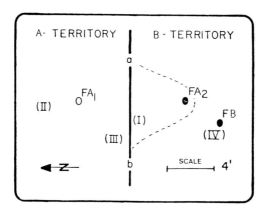

This diagram illustrates boundary relationships after a female renested in an adjacent territory. A female (FA) deserted her nest (FA$_1$) in A territory and renested in B territory (FA$_2$), placing a section of the boundary (a–b) in a questionable status. A caged young from the nest in B territory (FB), when placed at positions indicated by Roman numerals, drew the following reactions:

I. Male A and female A remained on the area enclosed by the dashed line when female B first visited the area to feed her caged offspring, but only female A offered any resistance. One minute later, male A withdrew before an attack by male B, and both male B and female B occupied the area.

II. Male B halted at line a–b; female B attempted to reach her young, but was routed each time by male A (and harassed by female A). Female B was unable to reach her offspring during 30 minutes of observation.

III. For ten minutes, female B was unable to reach her offspring. Male A remained perched between the young and its parents (male B and female B), facing them across the line a–b.

IV. Male B and female B at once visited their young without any interference.

in the territory of another pair, flew straight from the nest-box to their own territory, never perching anywhere else within the strange territory. Nest material was gathered out of the territory and neither the male nor the female ever uttered a note or displayed when the resident male visited their nest. The latter made no objection to their presence. "There *were* no boundary lines, for the strangers made no claim to land . . . all they wanted was the nesting box, for they had no suitable hole in their territory."

Wingra Marsh birds were remarkably faithful to their territories, returning year after year to essentially the same areas of the marsh. In an investigation in Washington of male Redwing characteristics and

Marsh Wren

harem size, William Searcy concluded that because of male site fidelity, males with the greatest competitive ability did not necessarily get the best territory and the biggest harem. Therefore, one could not conclusively say that sexual selection had a large effect on the evolution of male Redwings. Searcy found a lot of variance in his study and believed that a good deal of it could be explained by "historical accident rather than male quality."

"Historical accident" was certainly a primary factor shaping many events in the lives of Wingra Marsh birds, but there is another way of viewing this aspect. This amounts to the old question posed by human historians—is it the war or the times that determine events. Surely both the strengths of the bird *and* the situation in which he's placed (including the physical factors, but also the relative presence/strength of other birds) are important. Thus, behavioral factors begin to contribute to evolution along with sheer considerations of individual strength . . . even among birds.

Relationships with Other Birds

During my study, Redwings (usually males) were observed driving or attempting to drive the following species off their territories or from near by: Great Blue Heron, Green Heron, Mallard, Blue-winged Teal, Northern Harrier, American Kestrel, Belted Kingfisher, Northern Flicker, Downy Woodpecker, Eastern Kingbird, Common Crow, Black-capped Chickadee, Marsh Wren (an especially vigorous opponent), Gray Catbird, American Robin, Common Starling, Palm Warbler, House Sparrow (at the zoo), Common Grackle, American Goldfinch, Dark-eyed Junco, Tree Sparrow, and Swamp Sparrow. Both male and female Redwings were especially antagonistic towards grackles and Marsh Wrens nesting on Wingra Marsh. One belligerent female chased a Marsh Wren vigorously and even perched on the latter's nest. Redwings, on the other hand, were repulsed by an American Robin (at her nest), by Rock Doves (at the zoo), and by a Warbling Vireo that had a nest in a tree on the marsh. Curiously, three bright red male Cardinals were seen singing on Wingra Marsh at the same time; Redwings seemed completely disinterested in them.

Where Yellow-headed Blackbirds and Redwings occurred on the same marsh, Yellowheads, which are larger birds, usually dominated

Redwings. On one occasion, however, I saw a determined female Redwing drive a male Yellowhead away from the vicinity of her nest and beyond.

On April 27, 1951, when a Sharp-shinned Hawk landed on a tree in Wingra Marsh, male and female Redwings flew up into the air with alarm cries. As long as the hawk remained on its perch, the Redwings stayed aloft. On other occasions when Sharp-shins appeared high overhead, the Redwings flew down into the shelter of the cattails.

On two occasions I observed resident males engage in an aerial battle with American Kestrels, each time driving this raptor away from the territory and the marsh (not at Wingra). In May 1982, near Winnipeg, I saw a male Redwing move a Kestrel along telephone wires near a roadside marsh—three times it displaced the Kestrel.

At Wingra Marsh on March 25, 1950, a Cooper's Hawk landed in the trees across the road. It gave a strident *"kee, chi chi chi chi"* and remained perched. All the birds in the vicinity froze, especially an unbanded adult male Redwing on the marsh a hundred feet from the hawk. This bird had his legs spread wide, clutching two cattail stalks for support, when the hawk arrived. The Redwing remained in this ludicrous pose for at least thirteen minutes, the duration of the period the hawk was present. As soon as the hawk flew away, the male, which had held his plumage compressed all this while, shook out his feathers and burst into song. Other Redwings on the marsh at greater distances from the hawk had given song intermittently.

Relationships with Mammals

I had an unusual experience one day when I went to check a trap on the dike. To my dismay, I found the trap almost completely submerged in water. In it was a dead Redwing, one of the oldest resident males on the marsh, lacking only one color band. As I was taking the wet bird out of the trap, a mink suddenly appeared on the dike about six feet in front of me, nervously sniffing the air and making tentative forward motions, advancing in short steps. Was this the culprit, then? It came close to where I was kneeling and when I slowly and gingerly extended my arm with closed fist, it actually touched my knuckles with its wet nose! I extended my other hand, holding the bird out toward the mink. At once it made a quick jump forward and seized the prey in its teeth, hanging on tightly and trying to draw away; it wouldn't let go! I knew that weasels were bold and would return to prey despite the presence of man, but I hadn't anticipated such brash behavior from a full-grown mink. Jim Beer and Doug Tibbitts noted that in 1946 when a mink had a den in an old muskrat house on the dike at Wingra Marsh, only 28 young Redwings survived as compared to 170 young the following year.

Occasionally, when a mink moved through the cattails during the breeding season, most of the birds gathered overhead and harassed it until it had left the marsh. This kind of group or mob reaction is often seen when marauding crows appear near a breeding site, but it seemed more intense in the crowded situation at Wingra Marsh.

One of the longest observations of interactions with a mammal involved a pair of Redwings and a sheep. This was on July 2, 1953, in an alfalfa field on the University Farm close to our home in the Trailer Camp. This was an isolated pair of birds with one well-feathered young in a nest that had been knocked down flat on the ground, probably by a sheep, a few of which had been recently let into the field. When the grazing sheep moved toward the nest, the female Redwing called in alarm: "tsseek!" and especially "tch!"—and landed on the sheep's head. The equally alarmed male used the same calls and landed on the unperturbed sheep's nose. Both birds walked up and down on the sheep's head, flapping their wings and pecking, uttering alarm cries incessantly while the sheep looked at me with bland eyes and kept on chewing! One alarm call was given at least every two seconds during this curious situation.

Finally, after an hour, the sheep moved away and the pair of Redwings turned their attention to me. By this time the young bird had left the nest. Although the pair had previously directed all their attention to the sheep, the pair now hovered over my head. The female emitted a peculiar long, soft call: "heehh!" The male's call was higher-pitched, shriller, and louder: "heeuu!"—almost identical to the alarm cry of a young bird. This was given repeatedly, gradually sounding more and more like a young bird in distress, a fast "hew!" or "heeew!" It was not the first time I had noticed that adult alarm calls resembled extreme versions of the vocal efforts of young Redwings.

At Fish Lake, Wisconsin, on June 24, 1951, I saw an adult male Redwing drive two plow horses—great beasts—off its territory, where the horses had presumably gone to drink. The bird flew down onto the rump of the nearest horse and clung there, persistently pecking while the horse plunged landward.

In this connection, I can't resist quoting a fictional source, presumably based on some valid observation of Redwings in upland habitat in the Midwest. In a novel by Harold L. Davis I found the following descriptive note: "the hogs galloping frantically for the feed ground through the greenish-brown clumps of alfalfa, with blackbirds swarming overhead and some still clinging to their backs, teetering back and forth and leaning wide on the turns like jockeys rounding into the home stretch in a driving finish."

5

Courtship and Mating I

Polygyny

Polygyny, that is, having more than one mated female per territorial male, has been recorded in the Redwing by several authors, although a few observers have reported this species to be monogamous (one mate). Redwing matings at Wingra Marsh during my study were occasionally monogamous but were mainly polygynous. Of twenty-five males for which accurate records were kept, five had one mate, sixteen had two mates, and four had three mates. I had no record of a male breeding successfully with more than three females. However, in at least one case where a male had three mates, one female returned for a second brood, so that four broods were raised in this territory.

Jean M. Linsdale, working with unmarked birds in Nevada, reported as many as six females per male. Maurice Giltz told me that he found an average of 6.5 females per male in upland habitat in Ohio. Improbable as it may seem, Orians found one male Redwing with a harem of thirty-three females! He reports that this was roughly three times the number recorded for any other territory in his Washington studies.

According to Linsdale, "The success of a male in obtaining females in its territory seemed to depend almost entirely upon the suitability of the habitat for nest locations." My females showed a preference for nesting on edges of openings within dense cattail stands. Since not all territories had an equal amount of edge, some might have been more suitable for nesting than others. Linford, in Utah, found that territories of polygynous males were twice the size of monogamous males, but I found no relationship between territory size and the number of nesting females.

Allen considered that the male Redwing was not "agreeable" to polygyny because of the great difficulty of running two or three double families each season. He suggested that a male was "satisfied" with one female. However, the males in my study played little part in feeding the young and only a few birds (three) had more than one brood. Female intolerance of other females may play a large part in limiting the number of females breeding in one territory; and a male is rarely able to "court" successfully two females at exactly the same time.

Nesting data at Wingra Marsh tended to support this—in most, but not all, cases females within a single male's territory were "out of phase" with each other. Females maintained some dominance over a small area surrounding their nest, being more aggressive to harem mates than to strange females. (For more on female subterritory see chapter 8.) In upland nesting birds, Giltz told me, he found that under alarm cries harem mates would often show great tolerance of each other. Following the broadcast of a distress cry "the two or three females of a male's harem would not only tolerate each other but often stand together on a mustard plant or other weeds within their territory. 'They knew each other.' "

Polygyny in the Redwing is related to the fact that first-year males do not usually breed, whereas first-year females do, thus providing a population with a surplus of females. Marked first-year females were regularly observed breeding on Wingra Marsh. Female Redwings experimentally induced to breed in captivity with immature males produced infertile eggs. Larry Holcomb reported that female Redwings on his study area bred each year with no notable surplus existing as nonbreeding birds. Ronald Howard found a difference between upland and marsh-nesting birds; the marsh population exhibited a higher level of polygyny (up to five females per male) than did the upland Redwings. Upland-nesting females, it should be noted, obtained more of their food on the territory than did the marsh-nesting birds.

Second Nesting

As Beer and Tibbitts suggested, double broods were uncommon on Wingra Marsh. I found only three cases of double broods in my study (in 1949, all successful). In each case in which females had second broods, they bred with their original mates. A female that arrived on April 17 had fledged young on June 8, and nine days later (laying date uncertain) she had her first egg in her second nest (no female Redwing has ever been known to use a nest more than once). Another female, which left with her young on June 15, returned on June 28 and had her first egg on July 4, seven days later. A third female was feeding her fledged young until June 27, and on June 28 had her first egg in her second nest. In two of the above cases the pairs were never separated, the females remaining on or near the territory while feeding their first young. By contrast, in 1950, twenty marked females had successful first nests, but none of these females returned to the marsh for a second brood.

The Pair Bond

In the Redwing, as in the majority of passerines, the sexes form a bond for the breeding period only. In many species the members of the pair remain together until the young are self-sufficient, but Redwings appear to separate as soon as the female leaves the territory with the young. This is necessarily the case when the male remains on his territory with his other females, but apparently even monogamous pairs separate. Individuals of either sex have been observed caring for young off the territorial grounds, but I never observed a marked pair together caring for their young off the male's territory, or at least very far from it. The pair bond evidently lasts only while the pair is attached to the territory. I made many unsuccessful attempts to observe breeding pairs feeding together outside their territory. Mated pairs only infrequently left the marsh together to feed (the male usually returning first), although, as already mentioned, males often left in small groups and these birds sometimes fed close together.

In the Redwing, the pairing bond does not appear to carry over from season to season as it does in the Brewer's Blackbird. Several of my returning females remated with their former mates, but others mated with other males even though their previous mates were present. Nevertheless, females that reassociated with former mates seemed to establish themselves with less effort than did those that acquired new mates.

The Redwing sexes tend to remain separate throughout the non-breeding season. Males revert to flocking behavior as soon as they quit their territories. My marked males were often seen associating with other adult males at the Vilas Park feeding grounds in late July and August. Females also flock together at this time and move to uplands with the majority of the young. Segregation of the sexes was found by Brooke Meanley in a large roost on the Arkansas Grande Prairie. Male Redwings (and grackles) were roosting in erect cattails and blown-over sedge. Females only were roosting on a smartweed mat. The feet, tail, and lower underparts of the female Redwings were in the water. Patrick Weatherhead and Hamilton Greenwood, however, have found some males and females roosting together during spring and fall.

Arrival and Establishment of Females

Arriving females are generally fairly quiet and may only give soft *check* or *prit* calls. Single birds or small groups circle in the air over the marsh or perch nearby and sit quietly or give frequent tail flips until approached by males. Usually the appearance of a new female alerts the males within several hundred feet and various short calls, such as a *check* or soft *ticka-ticka* or shrill *tseee* are given. Some males may sing and fly down to their respective territories; some may stay on their perches; others may perch near a female. If a female remains in a tree, then the males, perhaps several of them, may fly up and perch near her, slowly hop along the branches toward her (usually with erect epaulets), and then fly down with song-spread to their territories. Often females flee at the approach of males; the latter sometimes fly after them for several hundred feet before returning to their territories. Sometimes these females circle the marsh before flying away, and occasionally they suddenly dive into the cattails.

When a female lands in the cattails all the males nearby usually move up to their borders nearest the female and perform song-spread broadly. The holder of the territory on which the female lands approaches to within a few feet of her to do this and then displays for several seconds after the cessation of song. This "after-song" pose is sometimes accompanied by the sexual call, a soft, whimpering "ti-ti-ti-ti. . . ." On some occasions, males hold their wings spread before they sing. At this time there may be comparatively little song from the owner of the territory. If the female approaches the male, he sometimes drops down to the base of the cattails, often onto the early spring ice, and struts around with wings extended laterally, sometimes rapidly vibrating them, while giving the sexual call. Sometimes the extended wings may be partially raised. This display was observed immediately after song-spread with the male perched on the cattails.

Females sometimes flew quietly into Wingra Marsh and remained perched near males without making any apparent sound or motion, appearing quite relaxed. Although these females might evoke a display in the male, they sometimes quietly flew away without being chased. Established females occasionally flew into the marsh without arousing any special interest from the males, which were apparently able to recognize them as one of their own or a neighbor's mate.

In many cases, formerly resident females appeared to arrive at the marsh late in the evening after most activities had ceased. A few were observed dropping right down into the cattails with little hesitation. These females were often found within an hour after sunrise the next morning sitting quietly on a male's territory, behaving like established females, that is, they stayed on the territory and sang to passing females. Some females showed much "tail flashing," or rapid spreading and closing of the rectrices, sometimes accompanied by slight movement of the primaries. (This occurs in both sexes, but is especially prominent in females.)

Although some females (presumably transient or young) often visited several territories in rapid succession upon arrival at the marsh, most resident females settled rapidly on the territory of a given male and remained there. A few, however, remained on a male's territory for several days and then visited several others before finally settling on one.

Once a female has settled on a territory and become paired she may receive little attention from the male, particularly if she remains quiet and low in the cattails. However, her quarrels with other females settling within his territory nearly always bring forth aggressive interference from the male. Sometimes the female follows the male around as he shifts about in territorial defense. She may alight a few feet away and slowly move toward him, which usually causes the male to retreat. A newly established female may likewise move toward an adjacent male for a few days, but often will draw an aggressive response from which she retreats.

At other times the male shows an interest in his mate by diving at her, displaying near her, and sometimes following her off the marsh. Occasionally, males follow their females as they circle high over the marsh or territory. (There are always surprises. On May 25, 1982, while attempting to obtain color photos for this book, Bob Taylor and I watched a male following a female, both birds circling upward until they were out of sight. I've never seen Redwings fly that high before. The male came down first, appearing as a speck but coming down in a precipitous dive, ending with a flourish of song-spread on the wing in slow flight onto his territory. The female dropped down seconds later.) These flights are generally silent and seldom accompanied by other birds. Generally the male keeps himself between his mate and neighboring males, meanwhile giving song-spread, especially when males approach his borders. He is always active in driving intruders from her vicinity. Such behavior may be seen throughout the season.

Pair Formation

Pair formation apparently begins (or actually occurs) when a female enters a male territory. The male appears to assume a proprietary interest in a female that stops in his territory and suitably stimulates him. In several cases, when a newly arriving female briefly visited one territory and then left to enter another, the owner of the first territory dashed in pursuit to bite or strike her. Ordinarily, this brings an errant female home. These curious reactions were repeated several times under experimental conditions involving a female dummy placed first in one territory and then moved to another. The first male persistently trespassed in order to strike the dummy in spite of vigorous attacks by the second male. The male thus appears to "claim" the female from the first moment, but the latter's interest appears to be mainly in potential nest sites. Newly arrived females sometimes fight hard and long to keep other females from encroaching on their territories.

By contrast, pair formation in the Brewer's Blackbird occurs gradually over a long period right up to nesting according to Laidlaw Williams. Males and females remain in mixed flocks throughout the non-breeding season, showing no interest in each other, but as the breeding season approaches they begin to show signs of pairing: pairs walk about together and males guard certain females. Pairing behavior is inconstant at first, gradually becoming more constant as lasting pairs form. When former pairs reassociate, as they often do, they show less inconstancy than do new pairs. (This is further evidence of keen individual recognition in birds.)

Inconstancy in Redwings before nesting is probably minimized by the territory system. Females attached to one male usually are driven out of adjacent territories by the male occupants; moreover, once a female has chosen an area for nesting she shows little inclination to search elsewhere. There is thus little wandering except on first arrival. The concept of gradual pair formation, therefore, cannot be applied to the Redwing. However, some strengthening of the bond undoubtedly occurs through association during the ensuing days of breeding, although it probably never reaches the level of that shown by the Brewer's Blackbird. The stronger pair bond indicated in the latter species probably results from the longer association of the pair.

Courtship

In many species of birds, one or both members of a pair may spend considerable time manipulating nesting material and going through some of the motions of nest building before actual construction of a nest begins. Margaret Nice has termed this behavior "symbolic nesting" or "symbolic building."

Symbolic nesting occurs in both sexes in the Redwing, but is more pronounced in the male. Since it is somewhat difficult to differentiate between symbolic nesting and the onset of actual nesting behavior in the female, I shall refer mainly to the male's activities. His sequence of behavior has been grouped under the terms "symbolic nest-site selection" and "symbolic building" (the former leading directly to the latter). This behavior occurs mainly from the arrival of the female on the male's territory until coition and subsequent egg-laying.

In symbolic nest-site selection, the male generally "crouches" (see chapter 3) near and slightly above the female, gives song-spread, then flies and clings to a clump of cattails, holding his wings up over his back ("elevated wings"). Sometimes he holds this posture for several seconds and may glance back over his shoulder toward the female, which often flies down near him. If the female comes, he may leave;

more often he slowly works his way through the cattails or "crawls," using his feet to move slowly away from her, still holding his wings partly upright. Then he stops, "bows" with beak between his feet, and bites at nearby cattail blades or breaks off bits that he manipulates in the manner of a female building a nest. Often the female quietly follows him through the same winding path and watches. This entire sequence, or portions of it, may be repeated many times. Usually, this behavior is performed for the mate, but on two occasions males presented fragments of it before strange females that flew low across their territories. The male's flight to the clump is slow and usually appears awkward, the wing-beat being below body level. Sometimes a male will continue this strained flight from clump to clump.

As the male hits a clump, he commonly utters a low, harsh, buzzing "hahh" or "shhh." This "growl" is often given in threat when the bird is harassing other species, immature males, occasionally his mates, and other females (?), but apparently not other adult males. (Females sometimes emit a similar call when driving off other species.) The call is quite long and is given with the bill open, sometimes remaining open for a short time afterward. Although generally a low sound, it is fairly audible and may be heard from at least a hundred feet. Although it may be given at any time during the sequence outlined above, the growl is usually given as the male peers into the cattails, either from the outside of the clump or as he crawls and bows within. On one occasion, a male came up out of a clump and faced his mate while giving this call.

Why does the male give a threatening call when peering into a potential nest site? Is it to reassure the female that this is a "safe" place? Amelia Laskey found that a male Mockingbird gave "a harsh rasping note" when it went into a potential nest site during symbolic nest building. And Niko Tinbergen reported that during the pre-oestrus period of the female Snow Bunting, the male and female frequently go about together inspecting little rocky crevices of the sort in which the female eventually builds her nest. He writes: "When entering a hole the male uttered a sound that to us was indistinguishable from the sound that was heard from a threatening bird. We did our best to detect a possible difference, because we did not expect to hear the same call in such widely different situations, but we must confess we did not succeed."

While the courting Redwing male clings to the cattail clump, his wings may be held completely erect, sometimes even touching over his back, but at other times they may be only slightly elevated and slowly flapped, or held out with only the tips shaking. In one case, a male raised and flapped his wings successively higher and faster as his mate approached him in flight. This observation and others suggest that the higher position indicates greater intensity. In one unique case a male that appeared to be unusually excited during an intense elevated-wing display uttered a series of short, high-pitched notes that increased in tempo and pitch to the end.

Symbolic Nest Building

Ordinarily, symbolic nest-site selection ends with the bowing movement in which the male Redwing bites at nearby cattail leaves. However, more elaborate sequences of pseudo nest building have been observed. In May 1950, a male was courting a female that had just come to his territory, although she had been present on the marsh for several days. This male displayed at the nearly completed nest of another of his females, which was absent at the time. While the new female watched, he *went inside the nest* and then *went through the motions of building,* forming it with his breast, lowering his head into it, and picking here and there, meanwhile holding his wings erect. Spectacular! After two minutes the female moved away from him. He went near her and then she followed him back near the nest and again he went through the nest-building behavior, although this time not in the nest. The female moved away from him again and then once more he led her back. Finally, he went up to the nest and, while the female watched, he lowered his head into it and then reached outside and appeared to pull in material.

You can imagine how excited and pleased I was to see this performance. This observation is of special importance since in many hours of watching I have never seen the male take part in actual nest building.

In another case, a female watched a male "play" at building. According to my field notes of April 21, 1952: "Male YRWX with spread legs [perched on cattail stems] in a good clump and with head down arranges bits of cattail about himself, picking and placing more or less for several minutes while his mate, XGGB, sits nearby." Noel Hackett stated in 1913 that the male Redwing helps construct the nest; I suspect he may have been misled by a male engaged in symbolic nesting.

In yet another case, a different male—after leading a new female into a clump of cattails—broke off some dead leaves and pulled at a piece of string that had been left there in trapping operations. When the female moved away from him, he went to her, bowed with raised wings and erect epaulets, and then *climbed up to an unfinished nest* nearby, where he gave the growl call. Then he *reached into the nest* and picked at the nest material. Later, this male went through the same behavior with this female in a cattail clump at a different place in his territory.

Such behavior by the male in a species where only the female builds the nest seems remarkable. A few cases have been reported, however, in which males of such species apparently constructed complete nests. William Dawson reported in 1923 that a male Hooded Oriole "was observed day after day as he constructed a nest on the underside of a palm leaf." And Thomas Nuttall wrote in 1832 about a male Northern Oriole building a nest. William Schantz tells how he watched a male Song Sparrow construct a complete nest in which a female later nested. In referring to the latter case in 1943, Margaret Nice suggested that the latent nest-building ability, appearing in most male Song Sparrows in the symbolic manipulation of material, developed through practice when this male was mateless for two years.

Symbolic nesting by the male apparently occurs in several other icterids besides the Redwing and the orioles mentioned above, in which the female alone builds the nest. Arnold Peterson and Howard Young reported that a courting male Common Grackle "repeatedly picked up and moved a bit of paper with his bill, replacing it in a crude nest consisting of a few twigs in a crotch about twenty-five feet above the ground. He frequently lifted his wings, spread his tail, and 'skreeked.' The female, perched about a yard away, also held a scrap of paper in her bill, but she remained more quiet than the male." Williams states that in the Brewer's Blackbird, "The male of the pair is sometimes the first to hold nesting material in the bill, but he rarely places it at a site."

Although symbolic nest building has not been observed in either of the meadowlarks, a hand-raised male Eastern Meadowlark showed nest-molding behavior. Mrs. Nice also observed nest-molding behavior in a hand-raised male Redwing at thirty-nine days of age. George Ammann quoted Irene Wheelock as stating that "she has known the male Yellow-headed Blackbird to make a pretense at nest-building a few feet away from the real cradle. . . ." And Ammann observed males of this species "casually pecking at a few strands of nesting material attached loosely to the reeds near finished nests."

I found a close similarity between Redwing behavior and that of the Yellow-headed Blackbird in Saskatchewan, and was especially delighted to observe a male of the latter species using an old nest in connection with symbolic nesting just as in the Redwing. On May 22 and 24, 1957, this male, which had been without a female, flew to the nest, picked at it, bowed into it, and showed excessive excitement and bowing when some females flew over the marsh. On May 24, at 6:05 a.m., my notes read, "He is on the nest! Gives song-spread, hops on the edge of the nest, lifts tail? Hops off and down into cattails."

Gordon Orians and Gene Christman noted for the Tricolored Blackbird a "nest-site demonstration" in which a male "works his way down to a nest site low in the vegetation and continues to display there, pointing his bill at the site, moving it back and forth rapidly, and sometimes picking up nest material. . . ." David Lack and John Emlen found the courtship display of the Tricolored Blackbird similar to that of the Redwing. My own review, in 1964, of symbolic nest building in icterids showed that many members of this group share similar behavior patterns for all or parts of the sequence. This suggests that it may be a basic pattern in this family.

Symbolic nesting in male Redwings, as well as in these other species, may represent vestiges of functional behavior from a time when the male played an active part in the actual activities of selecting a site and building a nest. Although in nearly all of the Icteridae the nest is built solely by the female, Herbert Friedmann reported at least one exception in cowbirds. The most primitive species, the Bay-winged Cowbird, is nonparasitic, but mated pairs locate and fight for the possession of nests of other species of birds, which they then occupy. Usually some alterations of the nest are made, and when no nest is readily available *they build their own*, the *male* generally building more than the female. And in the Shiny Cowbird, which is parasitic and normally builds no nest, both male and female have been seen attempting to build. William Beecher believes that the cowbirds are very close to the original primitive form, the buntings or Emberizinae, from which he considers the blackbird subfamily (Icterinae) to have arisen.

As to the possible functional significance of "symbolic nesting" behavior: in 1953 I observed that when I frightened an incubating female from her nest by jerking nearby cattails with a piece of string, her mate would often come in response to her alarm cries and fly down near her nest. When he withdrew, the female would return to her nest. This happened repeatedly. Sometimes when the male was absent or otherwise occupied and did not come to her calls, the female would fly about, scolding for several minutes, and would fail to return to the nest until the male arrived. The male's visit nearly always sufficed to quiet the female. Once when a female that was building the basal portion of a nest became greatly alarmed by the click of a concealed camera, her mate flew down near the partial nest and finally hopped right into it and peered about. These actions of the male somewhat resemble his behavior in symbolic nesting and suggest that the latter may have a "reassuring" effect upon the female as well as acting as a stimulus.

This interpretation is substantiated by observations of symbolic nesting by the male in "noncourtship" situations. During egg laying the female is irregular in incubation and the male, which sometimes appears restless or agitated when the female is not on the nest, may indulge in symbolic nest-site selection near the nest in what suggests an attempt to induce her return. One female had her first egg on the morning of May 28, 1950. I watched her mate from 5:15 to 6:30 p.m., while she was absent. Toward the end of this period, the male flew back and forth over his territory and finally went to the nest and "craned his neck to peer in. . . ." From 8:00 to 9:00 a.m., and from 6:00 to 7:00 p.m. the following day, the male went through complete sequences of symbolic nesting (even to the breaking of cattail leaves) near her, but especially near her nest (now containing two eggs). He visited the nest in conspicuous display attitude as if attempting to lead her into it. On the next day she laid her third and last egg, and again, from 5:00 to 7:25 p.m., her mate repeatedly went through "nest-site selection" behavior. When the female finally settled on her nest he flew to the other end of the territory, where he remained perched and quiet. On succeeding days she remained on her nest in more or less constant incubation and the male no longer showed the "courtship" behavior.

In another case (May 22, 1950), a female was kept off her nest by a trap that had been placed directly over it. The male went down near her, suddenly bowed, elevated his wings, and entered a dense clump of cattails, where he bowed and manipulated blades while the female watched from nearby.

During the egg-laying period or incubation, the males of many species perform nidocentric (nest-centered) displays directed toward their mates. I like the explanation offered in 1943 by Mrs. Nice: "A bird instinctively responds to certain situations; the situation egg-in-nest implies mate-on-nest-much-of-the-time; if the second element in the situation is not functioning he is disturbed; if his mate has disappeared he starts to sing (for her or another); if she is around, he tries to get her into the appropriate situation."

Female Choice and Polygyny

There is some controversy regarding the major attracting influences on female Redwings—is it the quality of the male or the quality of the territory? There is evidence that both factors are involved. Furthermore, the origin of polygyny is sought in these studies.

The titles of recent papers on these topics are indicative of the nature of the research; some are complex, a few are amusing. For example: "Male Behavior and Female Recruitment in the Red-winged

Blackbird" (by Weatherhead and Robertson); "On the Evolution of Mating Systems in Birds and Mammals" (by Orians); "Evolution of Polygamy in the Long-billed Marsh Wren" (by Verner); "Offspring Quality and the Polygyny Threshold: 'the Sexy Son hypothesis' " (by Weatherhead and Robertson); "Harem Size, Territory Quality, and Reproductive Success in the Red-winged Blackbird (*Agelaius phoeniceus*)" (by Weatherhead and Robertson); "Effects of Supplemental Feeding on Timing of Breeding, Clutch-Size and Polygyny in Red-winged Blackbirds *Agelaius phoeniceus*" (by Ewald and Rohwehr); "Polygyny and Female-Female Aggression in Red-winged Blackbirds (*Agelaius phoeniceus*)" (by LaPrade and Graves); "Female Choice and Polygyny in Redwinged Blackbirds" (by Lenington); and "Male Characteristics and Pairing Success in Red-winged Blackbirds" (by Searcy). There are many more titles in this area of research; it is an active field of interest to which the reader's attention is directed by reference to the above papers.

Studies of this nature are of considerable interest in that they are testing Darwin's viewpoint that the ability of males to influence the choice of mates by a female is a major force in the evolution of secondary sexual characteristics. It is a mark of Darwin's wisdom and insight that his theories are being tackled in so many contemporary Redwing studies.

6

Courtship and Mating II

Sexual Chasing

Aggressive pursuit of his mate by the male Redwing is one of the live-
liest events on the breeding grounds. With scolding, chattering notes
the male tries to catch the female, which flies a fast, erratic passage
over, around, and through the territory. It happens on every marsh,
every roadside territory—and is a distinctive sign of the breeding season.

Sexual chasing, or pursuit of the female by the male during the
courtship period, has been described for many songbirds and for a few
nonsongbirds. It has been noted in the Redwing by numerous observers from 1832 onward. Sexual chasing has also been observed in the
following icterids: Bobolink, Brown-headed Cowbird, Yellow-headed
Blackbird, and Wagler's Oropendola. It is rare in the Tricolored Blackbird.

More than one hundred Redwing sexual chases were recorded in
detail at Wingra Marsh or elsewhere. In nearly every case these chases
involved birds that were already paired. H. Eliot Howard, in his study
on bird behavior, wrote: "Sexual flight [or chase] is a certain indication
of pairing; I have never known a female desert a male once it had occurred." Sexual chases between pairs of Snow Buntings usually indicated that the birds "had mated and that the female would stay with
the male she had chosen," according to Tinbergen. Sexual chases in
the Brewer's Blackbird are believed to be part of the mechanics of pair
formation "since they occur more frequently in pairs forming for the
first time and apparently cease when the pair is formed." Pair formation in this species, however, is considered to be an extended process
occurring over a considerable period before nesting.

Sexual chasing in the Redwing is usually marked by aggressive
pursuit by the male and rapid elusive flight by the female. In their efforts to escape, females occasionally fly into obstructions and even
into the water. Sometimes the female stays within the male's territory, but often she flies out over neighboring territories. Occasionally,
these flights take her far from the male's territory, but she usually returns at the close of the chase. The chases are often preceded by signs
of sexual excitement in the male, and in most cases it is the male that
first springs into action, suddenly diving at the quietly perching female. In some cases, however, it seems to be precipitated by special

situations that bring the female into sight of the male. For example, the male seems to be stimulated by the appearance of the female carrying nest material, particularly when she carries it for a greater distance and more openly than is ordinary or necessary. Females in conflict call forth aggression by the male, and this may lead to sexual chasing. Various calls of the female, or simply her arrival on the territory after an absence, may evoke a sudden chase.

The ending of a chase is sometimes as sudden as its beginning, the participants often stopping shortly after they have begun. Usually the male is the first to stop and, as soon as he quits, the female stops fleeing, often landing in sight of the male and usually in his territory. The extreme development of a chase occurs when the male overtakes and hits or catches the female. This may occur in the air or on the ground, either on or off the territory. In seven observed cases the male hit the female or seized her by the rump feathers. In one case a male caught the female in the air and held onto her while both birds fell together some forty or fifty feet down into the marsh. Albert Hochbaum saw this occur once in the Mallard and once in Pintails.

A male Redwing sometimes uses his bill to hold a female by the rump feathers for several seconds as she struggles to escape. On one occasion a male was seen holding a female in this manner for more than thirty seconds while she struggled to free herself. In another unusual case, a strange male, which intruded on a territory to chase another's female, caught her by the rump feathers and then momentarily stood on top of her (female response not apparent). Seizure of the upper tail coverts or the rectrices of the female during sexual chasing has been described for the Reed Bunting by Eliot Howard (1929), for the Snow Bunting by Tinbergen (1939), and for the Canvasback by Hochbaum (1944).

J. CARSON
1983
©

There is some suggestion that female Redwings may threaten strange males that attack them, and in two unusual cases, females apparently fought back with their own mates (May 29, 1950; May 12, 1951). Ammann states that when occasionally a male Yellow-headed Blackbird caught a female after a sexual chase, the female vigorously resisted the male's attempts to copulate. Tinbergen, in describing sexual chasing in Snow Buntings, says that the "female tried to escape and fought with great perseverance" with her mate. And Eliot Howard noted in 1929 that Yellow Buntings, at the conclusion of a sexual chase, may face each other in the air, apparently fighting. Whatever the outcome of a Redwing chase, both members of a pair might be sitting quietly side by side seconds after its end. Similar behavior was observed by Frank Chapman in Wagler's Oropendola.

Copulation was never observed as the immediate end of a sex chase in the Redwing. However, on May 25, 1950, a male engaged his female in a chase and then, two minutes later, flew up to her again and mounted in apparent copulation, although she showed no signs of sexual readiness beyond sitting still. Eight minutes later, however, she showed extreme sexual readiness (complete precopulatory behavior) and then copulation clearly took place. In his final approach to the female, the male's posturing was more extreme than in his two earlier approaches. Sex chasing probably may be considered an indication of the female's unreadiness. Eventually, however, the female is ready, and then one might observe copulation closely following a sex chase, as described above.

Song-spread often accompanies chasing, occurring both before and, in part, even during the rapid flight. A call that resembles the middle phase of the "flight song" and that has been heard in other situations suggesting a threat function is often given by the male during the chase. This call is a high-pitched, loud and nasal *tch-tch-tch*, often repeated several times. It may be given before as well as during the chase.

Group Sexual Chasing

Often other males from neighboring territories join a chase of the type described above; it then becomes a group chase. Although the basis for a group chase is usually a pair, occasionally a female may become the center of a group chase in the absence of her mate. Even in the confusion of a group chase, it is usually her mate that catches and seizes her. In one case a male returned to strike his female a second time after a neighboring male had intervened to hit her.

Group chases are typically noisy affairs, all males involved tending to give rapid and repeated song and even some spread-display, while on the wing. At this time the typical *oak-a-lee* song is given quite hastily, so that the first part is slurred and the last emphasized. It is not clear just what causes other males to join a chase. They always appear interested in each other's chases, but do not always join them. The movement of others to join is usually general—when one flies toward a chasing pair, others follow. Group chases in the Reed

Bunting appear to be similar to those described above. Eliot Howard writes: "Owing to some seasonal organic change she is in a condition to stimulate and so to attract . . . as yet she has acquired no experience of boundaries, and straying, passes outside the dominion of her mate . . . she evokes in turn the sexual nature of each neighboring male; and they, on their part, become excited, and their excitement may terminate in the sexual flight."

I think that in the Redwing, at least, the group response may often be of a more general nature, perhaps akin to group flocking about a predator. In the course of one group chase, several immature males and females gathered in the vicinity. In some instances groups formed so rapidly that it appeared the males were responding to the chasing pair rather than directly to the female. The *tch-tch-tch* call mentioned above seems to arouse other males. Often, just after a chasing male gives that call, his neighbors fly to join the chase, meanwhile giving the same call. On at least one occasion I have seen males fly to join a chase when the pair was out of their sight behind shrubbery. These birds seemed to respond to the vocalization of the male. In a few cases males evidently were aroused by the calls of others' females.

The extended chase, low and over several other territories, usually, but not always, brings about group behavior. Sometimes neighboring males fly into a territory to join a chase limited to that territory. The stimulus to chase a female or to join a chase seems to vary depending on the particular circumstances. Males that join chases, it should be noted, are usually themselves in the midst of courtship with their own females, and hence leave their mates to jointly chase another's mate. The behavior of a strange male that catches a female is apparently the same as that of the mate.

Nuttall's statement in 1832 that during group chase the several males do not show any "jealous feud" with each other seems not entirely true. I think the great amount of song that occurs during the group chase is an indication of the mutual aggression of the males rather than a direct response to the female. Almost always, at the close of a chase, and often before, the male mate, or owner of the territory on which the group gathers, turns to evict his neighbors. Sometimes the pursuing male even turns away from his female to do this. However, this may not always be the case, especially when the chase ends, as often happens, on a foreign territory or even on a neutral area. What seems more remarkable is that other males that are approaching a chasing pair often turn back in flight when the chase ends.

Group chasing is evidently the kind that Nuttall and Audubon referred to. The latter's idea that the female Redwing receives the attention of a number of males in group sexual chase, and then chooses one of them as her mate, does not seem in agreement with present observations. Beer and Tibbitts also apparently had such chases in mind when they described a "teasing" flight, involving one female and several males, which purportedly ended in promiscuous copulation. They implied that this was a general occurrence. I have no observation of promiscuity in Redwings, but at the close of one group chase four males in courting postures briefly surrounded a female on the ground and then dispersed (but see page 98).

Period of Sexual Chasing

At Wingra Marsh, sexual chasing occurred between members of pairs in varying degree with no particular order of frequency or intensity from the first few days of meeting for at least as long as eleven days. In some instances females were with males on their territories for several days before chasing was observed. Sex chases occurred throughout the breeding period, however, owing to late arrivals, remating, and renesting. The period of chasing is possibly correlated with physiological and psychological changes in the female, for once copulation occurred, sexual chases were noticeably fewer or absent.

Tinbergen stated that in the Snow Bunting "weeks may pass, after the female has taken a mate, before she is willing to copulate . . ." and sex chasing occurred throughout this period. In a few cases, a recurrence of chasing was observed in Redwings just before a second nesting. In one case a violent chase occurred twenty-two days after a pair had fledged their first young.

The Meaning of Sexual Chasing

Tinbergen believed that sexual chasing in the Snow Bunting originated from attempts of the male to copulate: "When the female did not take notice of the male, that is, when she did not adopt the attitude of readiness, she fled, and a sexual flight originated." The fact that the female flees before the postures of the male is taken as an indication of her sexual unreadiness, since later, upon similar advances, she assumes proper copulatory postures and receives her mate. Eliot Howard stated in 1929 that: "the behavior of the male is a genuine attempt to complete the sexual act . . . eventually when he flies excitedly towards her and settles beside her, she stays, postures, etc., and copulation results." Margaret Nice considered "pouncing" in the Song Sparrow analogous to sexual chasing in the above species. (An actual chase does not occur in the Song Sparrow; when the male pounces on the female, the latter usually stands still and at times even fights back.)

According to Nice, "pouncing has no immediate connection with copulation . . . pouncing on the mate may be a technique of the male for impressing himself upon his mate . . . of making his presence keenly felt." Although sexual chasing in the Redwing is not connected directly with copulation, it is part of a pattern of actions and reactions which lead to copulation.

Precopulation and Copulation

During precopulatory behavior the female gives a long, rapid series of soft, high notes ("whimpering"). In low intensity the call is slow and these notes seem composed of two sounds: *tse-it* or *seek seek*, but later the speed of delivery increases and these become *tsee-tsee-tsee*. The rapid series may also gradually become slower and end with double notes. This call may be given alone, but ordinarily it is accompanied by rapid spreading and closing of the primaries and, to a lesser degree, the rectrices, while the wings are held close to the body. The

Redwing female precopulatory display is accompanied by wing flutter and a whimpering call.

whimpering call and wing flutter are usually given while the female is perched, sometimes quite high in a tree but usually on or near the ground. Occasionally the female displays in flight. This display is similar to the female "generalized display" of the Brewer's Blackbird as shown by Laidlaw Williams, and, as in that species, is used long before copulation begins. It also precedes the high-intensity display.

As the intensity of the display increases, the female leans foward and lifts her tail and wings, exposing the cloacal area. At high degrees of intensity the female sometimes raises her head slightly while whimpering and fluttering her wings. Complete readiness for copulation is indicated by both the tail and the head being tilted sharply upward with the beak sometimes held open. At this time the body is depressed, sometimes with the breast resting upon the ground or the perch. During copulation the female usually rests upon her tarsi with bill and tail still raised. In one observation, the female swung her tail to one side and clearly extruded her cloaca just before the male mounted.

The male reacts to the female's precopulatory display by first perching close to her in the "crouch" position. If her display is limited to the whimper and wing flutter, he may do nothing more and may pay little attention to her, but on one occasion a male approached while displaying and mounted a female that had been sitting quietly on the ground. When the female goes into full display, the male typically drops down to the floor of the marsh, flutters his wingtips while holding them out, either raised or lowered, and gives a soft, whimpering cry ("*ti-ti-ti*") somewhat similar to the female's, but not as loud and usually not as long. Then—and this is a dramatically beautiful thing to see—with erect and sometimes violently shaking epaulets, puffed-out plumage, lowered and spread tail, and lowered head, the male slowly, and often silently, walks stiffly toward the displaying female.

If the birds are in a tree, the male sidles along on the branch until he reaches the female. When approaching on the floor of the marsh he sometimes walks for several feet, awkwardly climbing over obstacles. On one occasion a male walked about five feet along the ground toward a displaying female and then, still fluttering his wings, flew up over an intervening cattail clump and landed directly on top of the female, which had been out of his sight. The late Alexander Wetmore reported a similar behavior for the Yellow-headed Blackbird; when approaching their mates, the males "clambered stiffly along, hobbling over masses of bent-over rushes, with heads bent down, tails drooping and back humped. . . ."

As the male nears the female he may begin to quiver his wings more and then raise them higher, especially as he mounts. Then he may flap his wings rapidly and sometimes may even hold them almost vertically while on top of the female. He may also do this before mounting her. In a few cases males approached with wings lowered to the ground and mounted the female without raising their wings. The male mounts the female from the rear, slowly moving around her to do this when he approaches from any other direction, since the female usually remains in a fixed position. He remains on top of her for a very short time, perhaps two or three seconds, and then steps off. Usually the male mounts only once, but occasionally he may mount again. However, I have never seen a male mount more than three times in quick succession. After dismounting, the male usually moves off without any conspicuous display, but occasionally he may continue to move his wings, even though walking away from the female.

During copulation the female is apparently silent and motionless; afterward she may call and flutter and sometimes preen. On one occasion the male left the territory shortly after copulation occurred and

A male Redwing gives a sexual display to a female "dummy" (mounted bird) placed on a cattail mat in his territory.

the female then went into precopulation display again, giving an even louder and more rapid whimpering call than she had previously given.

Wetmore, apparently observing copulatory behavior of the male Redwing, wrote: "one male . . . often slowly ran along the ground with wings partly spread and half-raised and epaulets showing to their fullest extent, a very pretty display." Winsor Tyler in 1923 wrote that the male Redwing "faced her with his wings partly spread and, although I was immediately in front of him, I could see practically the whole of his shoulder-patches . . . an actual courting maneuver . . . proved by the immediately subsequent action of the pair."

The precopulatory behavior of both male and female Brewer's Blackbird closely resembles that of the Redwing. Similar behavior has also been noted in the Tricolored Blackbird, the Yellow-headed Blackbird, and several other icterids. Female Redwing precopulatory and copulatory behavior and posture is similar in the Snow Bunting and many other songbirds.

Stolen Matings

Sometimes in nonpromiscuous species, stolen matings occur. Eliot Howard, for example, says this of the Yellow Bunting: "stolen matings . . . are by no means uncommon where territories adjoin and different females are in different stages of development; and despite the efforts of the owner to prevent it, a male will sometimes succeed—as far as one can tell—in reaching a sexual union." In the Song Sparrow, on the other hand, stolen matings do not occur, according to Margaret Nice. The famed writer-ornithologist Louise de Kiriline Lawrence wrote me in 1957 that she had once observed such an affair in the Downy Woodpecker. She went on to say that she asked the distinguished animal behaviorist Konrad Lorenz about the matter of stolen matings. He replied: "My dear, it happens in the best of families."

Despite Allen's hint in 1914 that there might be some promiscuity in Redwings, it remained for Beer and Tibbitts to state flatly in 1950 that "the hen probably copulates most frequently with the male on whose territory she has taken residence but, when she is sexually ready for copulation she will respond to the first available male." This surprised me since during the years I studied at the same marsh I saw no evidence of promiscuity. My females seemed fastidiously single-mated. Alas! Now, looking at my measured statements of fidelity, I wonder whether I overlooked some degree of loose behavior.

Ingeniously designed experiments in Colorado in which resident males were rendered sterile through vasectomy proved that many females still laid fertile eggs; females were clearly playing around outside the territories. A later study along the same lines in Massachusetts also revealed promiscuity, again related to behavior outside the territory boundaries. The evidence showed that promiscuity declined as the season advanced.

I have no record of a stolen mating in the Redwing, and still consider it unlikely, at least on the territorial grounds. Males do cross boundaries to harass another's female, and in one case a strange male even stood on top of the female. However, no copulation has ever been observed under such circumstances. Even at a later time, when the pair are about to copulate, molestation is absent or rare, although neighboring males may move up to their near-borders. Females generally are recalcitrant to strangers—and their mates are completely so.

This is well illustrated by an observation made off the study area at a place where plowed fields adjoined a small marsh. A resident female flew into the field to feed, several hundred feet from her territory, and was soon joined by a strange male. Seconds later she came flying back, giving alarm calls, with the male in close pursuit. When they reached her territory she flung herself into the cattails, and her mate, along with several neighboring males, drove the intruder away.

Conditions similar to a Roman bath and accompanying orgy, however, were observed in Ohio Redwings by Maurice Giltz, who wrote to me as follows: "On three occasions around four o'clock in early May, I observed bright pink to red breasted females gather in a group increasing in size to 45 females as they flew over an alfalfa field of 40 acres. These females flew to an adjacent old field beside a woodlot with brush and last year's growth of weeds emerging from puddles of water up to 80 square yards in size. The males in the area followed the females to the puddles and bathed with the females. There were alternating bathing and copulating of the whole group of birds, the males jumping from one female to another and all of them alternating in and out of the water. I concluded that promiscuity was rampant."

Redwing Perception

There is one incident involving use of a female dummy to elicit courtship behavior for a movie camera at Regina, Saskatchewan, that stands out in my mind as good evidence of the perceptual ability of the Redwing. I had had a dummy on a cattail stalk in a territory where it received the attention of the resident male. The latter went through almost complete sequences of courtship and mating, copulating with the dummy several times. When we had finished our work I retrieved the dummy and we walked away from the site, moving through knee-deep grass bordering the marsh.

Suddenly there was a stirring song behind me—I turned about in surprise to see the male in full display in the grass along our path, about fifty feet behind us. The bird maintained a continuous high-intensity display, wings fully expanded, epaulets flaring, giving all the signs of a sexually aroused male. I walked back to where the male was displaying to try to uncover the reason for his peculiar behavior and found the female dummy lying upside down and deep in the grass where it had fallen from my carrying bag.

Clearly, the male had formed an attachment to the dummy, had watched me remove it and *walk away with it*, and then he must have seen it fall out of my bag of equipment. Though lying upside down and deep in the grass it still provided a strong stimulus source. It is the occasional insight provided by an incident of this kind that makes one realize that birds have complex faculties.

7

The Nest and Nesting Activities

Nothing in the marsh would seem to be as secure in position as a Redwing nest. The female works with diligence and skill to produce a softly lined pouch firmly attached to old, dead, upright cattail stalks (or other plants, depending on the site), a highly suitable container for the fragile eggs and nestlings. It is open to the sky and to sun and rain, hence eggs and young must be protected and sheltered by the female. It must withstand wind and the growing pressure of hot and crowded little bodies pushing more and more as they grow to fledgling size. It is a masterpiece of adaptation to marsh or meadow habitat.

During the nesting period, when Wingra Marsh was fully occupied, the Redwings would remain fairly quiet unless I moved into the vicinity of their nests. Males and females could be brought overhead in a chattering flurry by a squeaking sound produced by sucking on my hand. They were consequently so upset they followed me about for a considerable period, usually until I left the marsh. (Of course, in most visits to the marsh I simply went straight to my observation post, trying to be inconspicuous.) An even greater distress is caused during the period when there are large young in the nest and fledglings nearby.

One adult male knew me quite well and would repeatedly attack me whenever I ventured near his territory, hovering and scolding, then dropping onto my head, actually piercing my scalp and drawing blood with his bill if I was bareheaded. Hence, I usually wore a cap and at times had the pleasure of walking through the marsh with a male Redwing perched on my head. (This also happened in Saskatchewan.) This aggressive male simply sat there, pecking vigorously while I slogged through the marsh. Once it followed me over to the west observation tower, several dozen yards from its nest, waiting for me to reach the top before renewing its attack. John Emlen was in the tower with me, so I let him wear my cap; we waited to see which one of us the bird would tackle. But it wasn't the cap it was after—the bird came right after me!

Apparently I am not the only human to have experienced such direct and persistent aggression from a territorial male. Back about 1950, Mel Ellis, a columnist for the *Milwaukee Journal*, wrote an item entitled "Blackbird Annually Battles Angler." In it he describes how a certain male Redwing on territory at a trout stream always harassed him.

The author with an aggressive territorial male Redwing perched on his head. (Saskatchewan Museum of Natural History)

"Big trout come hard enough in this day and age. It takes some concentration to entice a big brown out from beneath an overhanging bush. That job of itself can be nerve wracking without having a chattering blackbird bombarding an angler on the noggin."

Nests are built by the female alone, although the selection of a nest site may be influenced by the male, the latter indulging in conspicuous efforts to entice the female and often leading her into suitable sites. Often, too, the male goes through the motion of building a nest (see chapter 5) and may even seek out an old nest when he is engaged in courtship behavior, as if to show the female what he has in mind. Still, it is probably the female that decides where to build. The edges of cattail stands appear to be highly favored sites, allowing a female to fly low over water to reach her nest. Some territories at Wingra Marsh had little edge, thus females were forced to nest deep within solid masses of vegetation. These birds had to reach their nests by coming in from above.

Redwing nests are about four inches in inside diameter and four to five inches in depth. Ornithologist William Beecher stated in 1942 that the "inherited nesting pattern" of the Redwing seems to be the "suspending of a kind of hammock of plant fiber between closely crowding, stout stemmed stalks, upon which foundation the nest itself is constructed." Earlier, Arthur Allen noted that the "tough fibrous bark of the swamp milkweed" is used for this purpose. Nuttall also

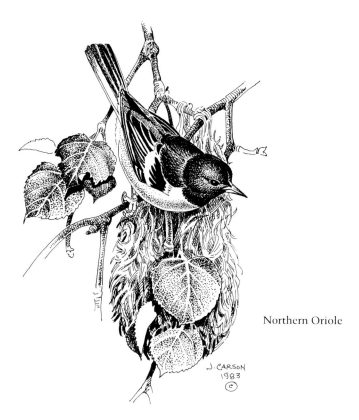

Northern Oriole

J.CARSON
1983
©

observed that the suspension for marsh Redwing nests often was composed of sedge leaves "sometimes blended with strips of the lint of the
swamp *Asclepias,* or silk-weed (*Asclepias incornata*)." Late nests may
lack this material, for there is a limit to the supply. It is the inner
bark, a fine silvery-grey material that wears loose in long threads,
available from old stalks of the previous years' growth that is used.

Some of the weaving skill of icterids that build pensile nests, such
as that of the Northern Oriole, may be seen in the silken platform
that the Redwing usually weaves as the first step in construction. In
Bent's "Life History" volume on blackbirds, orioles, etc., there are accounts of two pensile nests, including one found in 1883 that was six
inches deep, exactly like an oriole's nest.

One nest platform I found at Wingra Marsh was a complex cat's
cradle woven from white household string (left in the marsh by me),
using a piece about twelve feet long dexterously woven back and forth
and around the supporting structures. Another nest had an unusual
amount of milkweed fiber laid down in three successive layers. Not all
basal platforms are so well defined and I have seen one that was made
of bur-reed. I found Redwings in upland sites using fiber from the bark
of another species of milkweed (*Asclepias syriaca* L.), which grows in
drier, upland sites.

In contrast to the initial silken platform there is a bulkier basal structure to the nest proper, the "foundation platform" described by Beer and Tibbitts "built from coarse, wet grass." Bur-reed often served this purpose in nests I examined, but strips of cattail leaves are also used. Often, a peculiar sound heard on the marsh in spring is the tearing sound made by female Redwings as they pull off a strip from a wet cattail blade. In any case, old, wet and flexible material that dries to form a hard foundation is used. This is true of nearly all of the remainder of the nest. According to Beer and Tibbitts, this layer of material was left for a day before the next component, the "structural part of the sides" was built. This too was built from wet, old plant leaves.

Allen noted that the "felting" of the nest may be dead wood, decaying fragments of *Typha* (cattail) or mud." At Wingra Marsh I found birds using pieces of dead, decayed willow wood as part of the filling of the lower part of the nest basket, together with chunks of cattail. This all dried to form a firm, hard layer. Redwings nesting in upland sites near Madison, Wisconsin, used fairly large pieces of cornstalk pith, gathered when wet with dew, I suppose; it too ensured the formation of a firm bottom layer. It was an interesting substitute, for it looked similar, and dried in the same fashion as the pieces of willow wood used by birds on Wingra Marsh.

"On the third day," according to Beer and Tibbitts, "the sides are lined, followed by the completion of the nest on the fourth day by adding the lining to the bottom. The lining material is fine grass. . . . The process then starts at the top and works down as the lining is put in place."

Oliver Davie, writing in 1898, stated briefly that the nest was composed of "strips of rushes or sedges, lined with finer grass and sometimes with a few horse hairs." Harold Wood, who carefully dissected one nest, found it attached to eighteen bur-reed stalks, built of 142 strips of cattail leaves up to thirty-four inches long and making 273 laps around the reeds, only one making a complete circuit. Linford noted that there was a sling foundation of "tough weed fibers" and some horse-hairs in the lining. He astutely pointed out that hollow grass stalks have a tendency to straighten, thus forming a springy layer that lines the sides and stays in place. Stems on the sides of the cup are laid in circles, those on the bottom are crosswise. Often, when nestlings are lifted from the nest, they bring out the bottom lining clutched in their feet.

At Wingra Marsh, sedge stems were used for the lining; in the uplands, Kentucky bluegrass. Again, one has to marvel at the selection of materials that have the same form; despite differences in genera and species, basic forms function to provide the same results. It is as if the selection process were based on the nature of the material after it dries in the nest. In a study of the insulative quality of nests it was found that the nest cavity of the Redwing is "significantly deeper if the nest is 107 cm or more above the ground than it is at lower heights," according to Carol Skowron and Michael Kern. I presume this was related to different micro-climate temperatures.

If the nest itself is an example of the adaptability of Redwings to habitat differences, how adaptable are Redwings in making the change from marsh to upland nesting! It is this ability to nest in diverse habitats—from emergent vegetation in marshes, sloughs, and roadside ditches to upland meadows and thickets far removed from water—that makes them so abundant. Upland nests are placed on the ground or as high in trees as twenty feet.

Arthur Allen's comments about the tendency for early nests to be toppled by new growth are probably related to the fact that he was studying a cattail marsh that was frequently burned, thus removing most of the old stalks that would secure a nest. Such an occurrence was rare on Wingra Marsh, which was not burned.

According to Beer and Tibbitts, in a cattail marsh the nest "is located in relation to the 'apparent' height of the vegetation . . . that area that appears as a more or less solid mass and does not include the occasional stem that may go much higher. The reason for this location seems to be that the red-wing flies into the nest from above and the nest is located for this direct approach." William Francis notes that in Ohio upland habitat "selection of nest location apparently was independent of the height above ground, but was related to the distance below the top of the vegetative canopy in both species" (goldenrod and daisy fleabane).

"An analysis of eight studies of nesting success in Red-winged Blackbirds," Francis reports, "shows that there are significant differences in success among years, localities, ecological habitats and vegetation form. Differences in nest success as related to nest height, water depth, and time of initiating nests were not substantiated by statistical analyses."

A female may complete a nest in one day, skipping some of the finer points. Depending on the season, an egg may be laid the next day after completion of a nest or as much as ten days later. Beer and Tibbitts noted that at Wingra Marsh the average clutch in 153 nests considered to have complete clutches was 3.7 eggs per nest with a range of from two to seven eggs. The eggs are pale bluish-green, overlaid with streaks, blotches, and spots of black and brown. These latter markings, as pointed out by Linford in 1935, are water soluble; one can moisten a handkerchief with saliva and simply rub much of them off. I have found this true for eggs of many species of birds; it probably explains in part why the patterns on eggs gradually fade during incubation.

The usual period of incubation is eleven to twelve days, all the eggs hatching at once or nearly so. Incubation begins with the laying of the third egg, hence one of four young may be slightly later in hatching, and in larger clutches there can be quite a subsequent spread in nestling age. Larry Holcomb found that females would remain on artificial eggs for six or seven days beyond the normal incubation period.

Artificial manipulation of brood size in Redwings was carried out in New York. Nestlings from other nests were added to broods in experimental nests to determine the effects of increased numbers of young. "Despite greater within-brood losses, experimental nests produced more young than did natural and control nests," according to Cronmiller and Thompson. Nestlings in the enlarged broods, however, were lighter in weight than normal, probably because of the difficulty faced by the females in finding food. These results seem to fit the hypothesis that natural selection "produces clutch sizes that maximize the number of young that ultimately survive to breed and that the upper limit is set by the amount of food the parents can obtain for their young."

Although blind and helpless at hatching, the young grow rapidly. Even in the first day there is a noticeable increase in size. By the third day feather sheaths appear in all the feather tracts. By the seventh day the wing feathers have grown considerably. On the ninth day the feathers are well grown but do not yet cover all the bare spaces. The young birds can fly short distances, a few feet or so, if forced to leave the nest early. On the tenth day the stronger young may leave the nest by themselves and perch nearby.

It is the female that carries out all the duties of incubation and most of the feeding. Francis H. Herrick writes (in Allen's 1914 study):

In the space of four hours on the first day . . . fifty-four visits were made and the young were fed forty times. The female brooded her young over an hour, fed them twenty-nine times, and cleaned the nest thirteen times. [As in most songbirds the feces are whitish and contained in a marvelous membranous sac, so that it is an easy matter for the female to pick each one up and carry it away. I found a place in Wingra Marsh on the edge of a small shelf of green moss where a female had been discarding fecal sacs; there were at least twenty in the one spot.] The male made eleven visits, attending to sanitary matters but twice. . . . On the following day . . . in the course of nearly three and one-half hours, fifty-five visits were made, and the young were fed collectively or singly

forty-three times. . . . The male bird served food eleven times and attended to sanitary matters once. In the course of forty-two minutes, the first young bird to leave the nest was fed eight times, seven times by the mother and once by the father.

Allen notes:

The principal insects eaten are May flies, caddis flies and lepidopterous larvae. Generally three or four insects are brought each time, and one delivered to each young. This is not always the case, however, for sometimes the entire mass is given to one bird. There seems to be no order in this distribution, the young bird with the longest neck and widest mouth always getting fed first. The food is delivered well down into the throat of the young, and if not immediately swallowed is removed and given to another.

A detailed account of the food delivered to young Redwings at Wingra Marsh is presented by John Snelling who, borrowing a technique devised by Gordon Orians and his students, looped a one-inch length of pipe cleaner about the neck of the nestling tight enough to prevent swallowing of food delivered. "After about an hour the accumulated food bolus was removed and placed in a vial of 70 percent ethyl alcohol." Interestingly, "when white pipe cleaners were used eleven Redwings were removed from their nests by their parents. . . . Substitution of flesh-colored pipe cleaners solved this problem. It is suggested that the white objects in the nest released sanitation behavior of the female, in this case with adverse results."

"Though many of the cues by which blackbirds assess and select breeding habitats are still unknown," Orians writes, "they are apparently able to judge them well enough that the females approximate an Ideal Free Distribution in the Pacific Northwest. Females choose nesting areas primarily on the basis of habitat features rather than the characteristics of the males occupying them. . . . Marsh-nesting blackbirds share with other birds an ability to judge qualities of foraging patches and to shift their foraging activity in accordance with diurnal and seasonal patterns of prey availability. They do more sampling of different patch types at times of day when patches are changing rapidly in quality and, hence, it is less evident where foraging is best. Redwings reject small prey in Costa Rica, where they bring single items per trip to the nest, but do not in the Pacific Northwest where they are multiple prey loaders. . . ."

Wingra Marsh females were "multiple prey loaders," usually carrying several prey items each time they returned to the nest from a foraging trip. Of course, this varied with the size of prey, but generally they carried a bill full of larvae for the hungry young. I have always regretted that I didn't spend any time in a blind at a nest, where I could see the details of feeding behavior. Even with 7 by 50 binoculars, looking down from the observation tower, it was not possible for me to see things in detail.

Photographers, I think, must find special delight in working from blinds in order to get close-up photographs. The sound of young birds, the sight of waving open bills, and the hurried yet careful deposition of food in the gaping mouths by the female must afford memorable experiences.

A female Redwing feeds her young in the nest. (Dalton Muir)

8

Experiments with Nest Moving

Owing to the strong territorial drive of the male, Wingra Marsh females seldom wandered from the home territory, usually remaining near or on their nests, or, when feeding young, flying directly to and from the nest. From the day of their arrival on the marsh, females show much aggressive display to other females passing by overhead. Occasionally, two females within a male's territory may show some aggressiveness toward each other, but generally there is little opportunity for contact, and essentially none between females from other territories.

Standing on my tree platform on the edge of the marsh one morning, watching the females slipping through the foliage to their nests, I suddenly had an idea. I'd read about nest-moving attempts with other species; why not try it with Redwings? If it worked it might reveal new information about the relationships between harem mates as well as several other aspects of nesting that were poorly understood.

At the Zoology Department Animal House I found an unused metal can 18 by 18 by 24 inches deep with a heavy wire-screen bottom—just the right thing for what I had in mind for moving nests. The first nest I chose to prepare for moving was in territory A (see diagram [a]). It held four young a few days old. I sawed through the rhizomes of the cattail clump supporting the nest (A–1), raised the whole mass of dead and live vegetation, and floated it over and into the submerged can. I added a few stones for ballast until it was just right. The nest and its clump of cattails could now be towed through the water and left upright and stable wherever.I chose. All this, of course, while the owner of the nest, female A–1, was scolding and chattering all about me.

It was May 31, 1949, when I made the first move. I waited until female A–1 flew off the marsh for food, then quickly moved her nest six feet away from its original position but well within territory A (see diagram [b]). The nest clump looked natural, but was now in open water. As I climbed up to the tree platform to await results I felt excited and a little apprehensive. I was gratified when the female returned promptly with food and had no trouble finding her nest despite its new location; no particular excitement was evinced by either female or male. This at once suggested further possible moves, but I thought the female should have a chance to adjust to the new site.

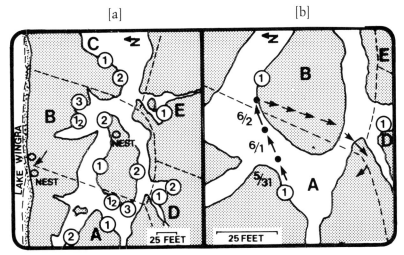

This diagram shows (a) the location of five territories and their nests before experimental nest movements (shaded portion is vegetation, unshaded is water). The nest-moving experiment is depicted in b. Nest A-1 was moved in a series of stages across open water and a territorial boundary and was left in B territory (see text). Continuous arrows show the route of return of the young after fledging.

I left the marsh greatly exhilarated, anxious to describe the results of the nest-moving experiment to John Emlen, "Doc" as we called him. His enthusiastic questions and suggestions for further experiments gave me strong incentive.

The next morning I waited until female A–1 left the marsh and again I moved the nest through open water six feet farther within A territory. Now it was twelve feet from its original site. Again, when the female returned, she had no difficulty finding the nest. This surprised me, but it boded well for the success of additional moves.

A critical move was planned for the next day—a move of another six feet that would carry the nest across the border into an adjacent territory (B). This was carried out on June 2 at 1:30 p.m. in the presence of female A–1 to ensure that she was aware of the nest's new location a few feet across the boundary separating territories A and B. Male A and female A–1 (the owners of the nest) moved immediately to the territory boundary where they stopped, male B being on his lookout perch, alert and nervously twitching his tail. At 1:35 the resident female, B–1 (her nest was six feet from the experimental nest), in her excitement over the disturbance, strayed across the boundary into territory A, where she was promptly repulsed by male A. The excitement continued unabated during the ensuing hour; neither female fed their young although both visited their own nest clumps. At 2:40 the resident and invading females (B–1 and A–1) fought on territory B; female B–1 won.

During the next half hour the invading female, A–1, reached her nest four times but was driven off each time by the resident female, B–1, and twice by the resident male, B. The invading female succeeded in feeding her young for the first time two and one-half hours later at 3:00 p.m., the defending birds having relaxed somewhat in their persistence. A–1 fed her nestlings irregularly during the rest of the day, often under attack by both the resident male and female.

On June 4, when I was next able to visit the marsh, I found that the four young from the transported nest (A–1) had fledged; two of them were back in territory A, presumably having crossed open water. The other two remained quiet and undisturbed near nest B–1. I then replaced the two young that had reached territory A, near their nest, in territory B for further observations. The mother bird (A–1), rather than cross a wide expanse of open water with her newly fledged young, led them in a roundabout route skirting the territory boundary and invading a third territory (D) before returning with her charges to her home territory. During this activity, the proprietors of territory B did not interfere, their aggressiveness apparently having subsided. Upon invading territory D and the vicinity of nest D–1, however, both the female and her young were promptly attacked by male D and female D–1; and the mother bird was chased back into her home territory. In the excitement, male D crossed three times into territory A, where he was promptly driven back by male A, which watched closely but never invaded his neighbors' territories.

Never were territorial boundaries so well demonstrated. Two of the A–1 fledglings hid in territory D, and their mother was unable to get to them for several minutes because of the attacks of the resident birds, particularly the male. At 12:00 noon, the brood, after further harassment, crossed the boundary into their home territory (A) and were no longer attacked. I left them there; they'd had more than enough stress.

On June 7 I transported a newly fledged young from the invaded female, B–1, into territory A. This young bird remained quiet and was not attacked, but the mother, B–1, was vigorously repulsed by male A when she trespassed over the territory boundary to feed her offspring.

In another experiment in July, second nestings in the same two territories provided an opportunity to perform an almost complete reverse experiment. A nest with eggs from B territory was moved by stages forty feet over the boundary into territory A (diagram [a]). Essentially the same results were obtained. Female B–1(2) (her second nesting) accepted her nest at each new location, finding it fairly quickly upon her return to the marsh. On one occasion, when the nest had been moved ten feet, she first visited the former site, then the original site, and finally the new site, which she accepted.

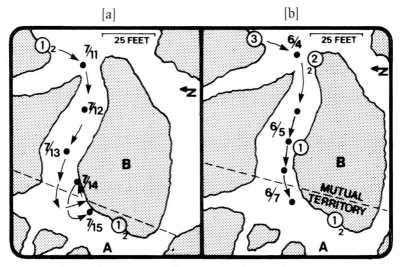

Diagram a depicts the experimental movement of a nest from territory B into territory A (see text); diagram b shows the movement of a second nest from territory B into territory A. (See text for results.)

As I approached the boundary of territory A, I moved this nest in five-foot stages. Although initially male A showed only mild alarm when the nest finally moved across his boundary, when female B–1(2) perched conspicuously on a clump of cattails, he immediately attacked and routed her. Several times in the next forty-five minutes she attempted to reach her nest, but was driven off by male A. The nest was then withdrawn from territory A and the female settled on it for the night.

On July 15, I moved nest B–1(2) to within fifteen feet of nest A–1(2) (a second brood) in territory A. Female B–1 soon approached the nest, going in low and quietly and from clump to clump. Female A–1 showed no aggressiveness except for quiet scolding when female B–1 flew directly over her. Male A once kept female B–1 away from her nest for five minutes, and another time chased her so vigorously she hit the water in trying to escape. Male A continued to harass female B–1 occasionally, but with diminishing vigor. On July 19 he even attacked her at the nest. Despite these series of incidents and the various displacements of their nests, however, both females successfully fledged broods.

In the third major nest-moving experiment, I moved female B–3's nest (two eggs, two young) several times beginning June 4 (diagram [b]). On one occasion I moved her nest fifteen feet while female B–3 was away from the marsh looking for food. Upon her arrival back at the marsh she looked for her nest where she had last seen it, then visited nest B–2(2) (renesting) and apparently dropped her food in with the four eggs in that nest. A moment later female B–2 drove her away. After a few minutes B–3 found her nest and soon flew off for food.

Two days later I moved nest B–3 eighteen feet in a series of stages, allowing the female to find her nest each time. Eventually, the nest was moved into territory A during the absence of male A. When male A returned and saw female B–3 he immediately drove her back to territory B. Keen individual recognition was apparent. Male B offered no assistance, but scolded from nearby. From then on, female B–3 approached her nest cautiously, coming in low and slowly. Although chased by male A on several occasions thereafter, female B–3 successfully raised her young at this site.

These experiments in nest moving showed that male territorial boundaries were sharp and stable throughout the period of nesting, as generally noted by others. Males recognized the boundaries of adjacent territories and were reluctant to cross over them. In cases where nest moving accentuated border defense, boundaries could generally be drawn within a foot or two. The territory boundary, at least where territories adjoin, are mutual, or common, boundaries.

Males defended their well-defined borders against invasion by other males, alien females, and alien young. Exclusion of other males is usual among territorial birds, but aggressive repulsion of females and young by territorial males is unusual in sexually dimorphic species. In Redwings, a territorial male differentiates sharply between females of his own harem and those of his neighbor's. Alien fledglings were generally driven from the territory, but in four cases they were tolerated. Along with this stiff defense of territorial boundaries, the male Redwings under study at Wingra Marsh showed a definite recognition and respect for the boundaries of neighboring territories. In no case did males attempt to follow nests transported out of their own territories nor did they offer any assistance when their mates were persistently attempting to penetrate the defense of a neighboring male to reach their nests or young. Often a male would approach the boundary of his domain only to stop and face his neighbor, a foot or two away, in threatening posture. Doubtless the Redwing territorial system serves to reduce confrontation and fighting among males.

Females generally restricted their movements on the marsh to a portion of their mate's territory. Female recognition of male boundaries seemed to be a specifically learned response to a local situation. When drawn into strange territory by experimental nest-transplanting, females assumed a subordinate attitude toward the residents and were invariably defeated, whether these were males or females.

In summary, males were never tolerated on a territorial holding. The repulsion of females other than mates appeared to be nearly as definite and inflexible as the repulsion of males. Males generally repulsed strange females in a nesting stage (but courted females newly arrived at the marsh or birds deserting a territory and seeking renewal of mating with a new male) or with young. However, the barriers of exclusion were partially or temporarily lowered to quiet and inconspicuous females and fledglings.

The nest-moving experiments indicate that the nest carries more significance to the female Redwing than the nest vicinity as such (and see below). Nests moved to a new site in the presence of the owner were quickly discovered and promptly accepted. It took females a little longer to find nests moved in their absence. Females freely followed their nests as they were moved experimentally through the territory of the mate, but assumed a subordinate attitude and followed with some difficulty when their nests were transported across territory boundaries. Females took no part in defense of the male territory (against males), but opposed the encroachment of alien females that persistently invaded their territory to reach transported nests. Harem mates (female residents of the same male territory) tolerated each other at close quarters after nesting had gotten underway, but repulsed actual visits to the nest. Neighboring harem members tolerated each other after they became acquainted.

In 1950 I discovered a new technique for moving nests that further emphasized the significance of the nest to the female. The nest-in-a-can technique was suitable for moving nests located at or near the water's edge, but was of no use for moving nests built well within a bed of cattails. I made a wire-screen basket—just large enough to hold a nest—attached to the end of a forked stick. The idea was to remove

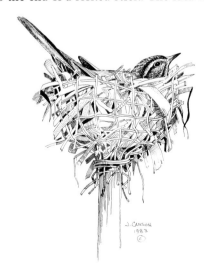

a nest entirely from its cattail supports and place it in the basket;
thus, it would be possible to put the nest almost anywhere and with
no lost time. I tried it. Within a few minutes after pulling a nest loose,
inserting it into the basket and planting the stick upright in the cattails, females with eggs promptly returned to incubation duties. It was
strange to see a female sitting up there fully exposed, crouched on top
of her nest in the wire basket.

I was all prepared to make a dozen or more basket sticks and
move nests to test other aspects, that is, exchange of nest with eggs
for one with young and vice versa. Sadly, one night most of the nests
in the marsh were raided, probably by a raccoon. Thus, overnight the
Redwings lost eggs and young and I lost the opportunity to carry out
the planned series of nest-moving experiments.

Frank Peek and colleagues, however, were able to carry out a series of experiments in which nests, eggs, or young were moved or interchanged. Their results prove that females show a strong attachment to nest sites "even though the nests, eggs, young (under 7 days old) were replaced with counterparts from other Redwing nest situations. When young older than 10 days were displaced from the nest site, females abandoned the site and followed the young. Female Redwings therefore learn to recognize their young during the period they are in the nest. The earliest that females were found to show signs of recognition was 7 days post-hatching. This recognition is probably based upon the location call which is given only by older young. Though the structure of the location call remained the same from one utterance to the next for an individual, it differed markedly between individuals."

Larry Holcomb, who also carried out a series of experiments involving transfer of eggs and young, found "no great differences in ability of females to accept any age group [nestlings]. However, during the egg-laying period most females fed nestlings sparingly and sometimes were aggressive toward nestlings."

Moving nests gave me a curious sense of deep involvement with Wingra Marsh Redwings. The physical act of moving about in the marsh and towing a nest through open water to a new site, the birds all nervous and scolding, the uncertainty, the tension of waiting for the return of a female whose nest had been displaced in her absence—those were wonderful moments. I was delighted with the quickness with which females found and accepted their relocated nests. And nothing was more exciting than the strong and immediate demonstration of fixed territorial borders. Perhaps most moving of all was the gradual acceptance of a foreign nest and female by the owner of the territory, demonstrating a flexibility of behavior, a capacity for tolerance. Clearly, birds are more than little machines.

9

Adult-Young Relationships

Females play the major role of feeding the young, both in the nest and out. In fact, it is with the females that the fledged young first leave the marsh to feed in upland habitat. Arthur Allen's work on this species showed that the young remain in the nest for nine to eleven days, the entire brood leaving at nine days if disturbed, but the weakest remaining eleven days if undisturbed. I calculated nine days in the nest for the entire brood, two weeks on the marsh as fledglings, and another two weeks off the marsh in upland sites with the female. Thus, the young are dependent upon their parent, or parents, for five to six weeks.

Female parents lead the fledglings off the marsh at an early age, almost as soon as they are capable of flight. In one instance, a female from the territory in which I had my tree platform led her young away from the territory one morning, always staying in front of them, sometimes holding food as a reward, eliciting begging calls and a following response. The male assisted in leading the young away from the territory. The female and young birds crossed the road into the woods, undoubtedly making their way slowly to the nearest uplands.

Both male and female had difficulty at first moving the young across an occupied territory, for resident males don't take these intrusions lightly. Initially, three young were gathered in a vacant territory and eventually all were safely herded across the road and into the woods. The male in this case came back at once and remained on territory. He had two good reasons for doing this. One, he had a second female nesting in his territory, and two, the youngest fledgling had been unable to make the journey, being too small and weak to fly along with its nest mates. This young bird remained in the care of its male parent for the next two weeks. During this time the young bird begged from the male and followed him about, sometimes even off the territory. At times, when the youngster was hungrier than usual, he flew up near the male on his perch and begged. Then, when the male flew off to look for food, the young one followed him off the territory. It soon gained flight confidence and occasionally circled about the marsh by itself, drawing aggressive action from each male as it crossed boundaries or landed in foreign territory. The young bird soon learned that it was safer staying on home grounds.

It was fortunate that I was watching this territory on June 28, for early that morning the original female returned. I even saw her arrival. As she "parachuted" down across the tops of the trees heading for the territory, her mate, evidently having recognized her at once, went into a full display, giving hearty song and spreading his wings and tail to the utmost—after all, he hadn't seen her for two weeks! And I don't suppose he had any notion that she was coming back. His splendid display, which welcomed her, also drew the attention of the young bird, which had been quietly perched nearby. The latter seemed to assume that the display was all for its benefit and it approached the male with begging gestures. At once, for the first time in two weeks, the male turned on it and repulsed it with an aggressive peck! The male clearly had his priorities in order. Still, the ever hopeful youngster hung about, presumably not knowing what else to do. The male, having settled into a strong renewed relationship with his number one mate, now turned his attention to the still persistent young. He deigned to feed it and attempted to lead it off the marsh, repeatedly trying to lure it away. It was still hanging about the next day, however, and eventually managed to get the male to feed it one more time. This was the last time; that day the young bird departed by itself and was not seen during the remainder of the season. Meanwhile, the male courted the female and eventually she had a successful second brood.

Allen, who studied Redwings at Ithaca, New York, recorded double broods far more often than we did at Wingra Marsh. He noted that "After the second brood has left the nest, which may be as early as July 1, the females and young gather in flocks and visit the uplands."

As mentioned above, fledglings are usually not permitted to trespass on strange territories, each resident male behaving aggressively toward them. This applies to young both flying low over the cattails and landing. Young birds that are able to fly well enough to circle at some height over the marsh are allowed to do so without interference. The vertical aspect of territory ought to be studied further. Generally, there is a height at which all but challenging males are ignored, but I know of no measurements of height tolerance.

Once attacked or menaced, young birds fly back to their home territory or to neutral ground. Actual attacks consist mainly of a male gently striking the youngster on its back so that it is forced to land or retreat. Males also do this to their own offspring to keep them within the home territory, or within the marsh, as noted by Beer and Tibbitts. Often, a fledgling will be attracted by the sight of its male parent flying low over his territory and will follow the latter down to a suitable place in the cattails.

Once, while demonstrating male response to a female Redwing dummy for a field class in ornithology in the summer of 1965 at the

University of Minnesota's Lake Itasca Biological Field Station, we were treated to an unexpected incident. I had set up the dummy in cattails at what I presumed was a point well outside a male's territory. The keen-sighted male soon flew over to visit the dummy, giving full song-spread displays and fluttering its epaulets in a state of high excitement. Suddenly, a fledgling took flight over the cattails back in the male's territory. At once the male turned and flew directly back home where he proceeded to pounce onto the back of his still-flying offspring, causing the latter to tumble down out of sight in the cattails. Then the male turned about and made a fast direct flight right back to the dummy, where he resumed his courting behavior.

It was a good example of a bird responding to a stimulus of higher priority (the flying young), then, on the instant that situation was back in order, returning to the stimulus of the dummy. Several minutes later, after I had retrieved the dummy and led my amused class over to the van (we were due back at the Station for lunch), the excited male had returned and was forlornly displaying at the spot *where the dummy had been.* He was still looking for the female as we drove away!

One windy afternoon while in a boat on a small lake several miles north of Madison I was surprised to see a segment of a cattail stand, a veritable table-sized raft, drifting downwind across the lake. It had evidently been torn loose from a cattail bed in a shallow bay at the other end of the lake. As it floated past I could see that it carried a male Redwing and at least one fledgling. I've always wondered about the outcome of that incident. Presumably the male tended the fledgling, until it was capable of looking after itself, and perhaps even led the youngster back to the original territory. That a male would look after a fledgling is no surprise, for the family bond is strong.

I was fortunate to find a few males at Vilas Park on the north side of Lake Wingra caring for young evidently left in their care when the females left the marsh with their broods. Two banded birds, twenty-seven days old, were found with their banded male parent on August 6, 1948, in company with about four dozen adult males. The male, RXRR in my notes, had been seen on the marsh until July 23. On July 31, the male was found at the park, along with seven other color-banded males. I did not witness him visiting the marsh again that season. Earlier he must have led the two young from the marsh across the lake to the park.

My field notes reveal some interesting aspects of the relationship of this male and his young:

Aug. 6—8:30 a.m. (young 28 days old). Young RWWX is found accompanied by [adult male] RXRR. The young appears to be a female. It is fully feathered, pecks about by herself, but obeys orders of parent as to when to fly and where. 2:00 p.m. The second young, a male—RBWX, is seen with . . . RWWX. Both accompany RXRR who feeds them and moves them about rather cautiously, giving me the impression of trying to avoid my staring at them. RWWX begs from an unbanded adult male who does not respond. She pecks about by herself and begs from every adult male that flies near her, but none respond. She approaches a grackle who munches a piece of white bread. She holds her head up with her mouth open but does not make any sound and does not flutter her wings (as she had previously done to the Redwings). She is finally led away to a fence and fed by RXRR.

Aug. 8—9:00 a.m. (young thirty days old). RWWX, RBWX, and RXRR, together with several other adult males, are found feeding on the lawn in the park. The two young peck about by themselves, but RXRR shows great concern over them. As I approach, all the males give the alarm "chk" and then fly away or up into nearby trees, leaving the young behind by themselves. The young keep looking about, but finally fly away together and perch in the top of a tree.

Aug. 12—1:00 p.m. (young thirty-four days old). RWWX is seen drinking water. RBWX begs in vain from an unmarked male, with RWWX nearby.

1:30 p.m. Both of the young fly after an unmarked male adult and then RBWX begs from him (in the horizontal position), but in vain. At this the adult leaves without giving the warning call given by their parent. The young remain behind and feed on insects. RBWX calls "cha-cha-cha-cha" and flies away, and RWWX follows. Later RWBX is seen begging from RXRR.

2:00 p.m. RBWX follows RXRR wherever he leads. He flies close behind him, lands near him, begs horizontally, picks up a leaf, drops it. The adult, RXRR, seems extremely wary, especially of me. He leaves with a "chk-chk" and RBWX follows after him. This same occurrence is observed six times in the next twenty minutes.

2:15 p.m. An unbanded female adult feeds an unbanded juvenile male who is larger than RBWX. The latter is meanwhile feeding or pecking about by himself nearby. RBWX shows aggression to the adult female, and that female obviously keeps out of his way. All three of the above birds were close together during this incident.

2:30 p.m. RWWX feeds herself on bread, although giving the begging call "chack" now and then. 3:00 p.m. RBWX feeds himself. . . . He seems to show more begging behavior than the other youngster. RBWX flutters over the water of a shallow pool. He steps in on the edge and drinks. He steps in farther and eats from some floating bread. He scratches his head by reaching from under his wing. He dips his head in the water and flutters both wings at the same time while holding his tail spread. Meanwhile he is quite wary. He performs this activity six times in three minutes. He sits up after he dips and gives a brief flutter with his tail held in the water, then flutters his wings over his back. He sits in the sun nearby and preens.

Aug. 15—9:30 a.m. (young thirty-seven days old). RBWX feeding himself. RWWX flies away calling "cha-cha-cha-cha" and RBWX follows after her. They appear always together and seem to keep in contact with such calls; each leads the other at various times. Both are feeding by themselves.

10:00 a.m. Both RBWX and RWWX beg from RXRR, their male parent, and

Female wing-flipping—a peculiar display given in response to the close approach of the male when the young are out of the nest.

follow him about the zoo. They seem to recognize him in flight or by his call. They both beg from him (horizontally) with fluttering wings while up in the trees.

No further observations were made of this trio.

I don't suppose anyone watching me had any idea of the excitement I felt observing and recording the activities of this color-banded father, son, and daughter. The gradual waning of feeding by the male, but still a bond between young and adult as well as between the juveniles, the casual way they were ignored by other males—all this was new information.

Female Wing-flipping

During the period of "feeding-the-fledglings," the female Redwing frequently raises or flips one or both wings when her mate is nearby. What does this signify? Such "wing-flipping" involves movement of the whole wing at body level and, at high intensity, nearly vertically. In some cases the wing on the side toward the male was held highest. Wing-flipping was observed to be given as much as ten feet from the nest, although it was also seen at a lesser distance. It was given especially just after a return to the territory with food for the young, and shortly before departure for more food. In one case a female flipped her wings before feeding her young and then kept them raised while actually feeding them.

At the Vilas Park feeding grounds several observations were recorded of females *lowering* a wing to the ground when approached aggressively by strange adult males. The latter usually behaved antagonistically to females on the feeding grounds. Once, when a female was threatened by an adult male, she raised and fluttered her wings at her sides in the manner of a young bird begging for food. The above behavior by females appears to be defensive. According to Margaret Nice, male Song Sparrows attempting to invade a territory often held one wing straight up in the air and fluttered it as they faced the defending resident male. In one unusual case, when a female Song Sparrow (which sometimes drives off trespassing birds) faced a trespassing male, she was "all puffed out and *flipping a wing*" at the male. It is a signal, perhaps, like waving a white flag.

Observations under normal conditions at Wingra Marsh were supplemented by observations at Regina, Saskatchewan, in 1955 during an experimental attempt to elicit wing-flipping for photographic coverage. On July 16, five newly fledged young from one nest were placed in a small cage that was set about twelve feet in front of the camera. For one and a half hours the female attempted unsuccessfully to feed her young, meanwhile giving extensive wing-flipping before the thoroughly alarmed male. The female frequently raised both wings, often holding the one on the side toward the male higher and rapidly reversing wings when she changed position. Much of this sequence was suggestive of the behavior of fledglings begging for food. The female continued to show wing-flipping as she searched for food as much as fifty feet from her young and the male, but her wings were held highest when the male was nearby. Sometimes one wing would be raised over her back and tilted over the opposite side . . . it looked impossible to do.

Wing-flipping by the female Redwing seems to be an indication of her concern with "feeding-the-young." Just as the male simulates nest-building behavior during courtship (see chapter 5) and in moments of anxiety during that stage of the cycle, so the female simulates exaggerated gestures of the behavior of hungry young.

Aspects of Nest Success

Raleigh Robertson, writing in 1973, compared several factors relating to nestling success in marsh and upland habitats. Growth rates were the same, with birds in both habitats reaching the same mean weight at fledging. "It is suggested that the relative abundance of food is approximately the same for nestlings in either marshes or uplands, but that a higher absolute abundance of food in marshes makes large,

A closeup of a young adult female in the fall. Note the pinfeathers behind her eye. (Robert R. Taylor)

dense colonies possible. The relationship between nesting density and food supply is not simple because obvious differences in the phenology of vegetation used as nest support are also correlated with colony size and density."

Age-related differences in the success of female Redwings were studied by Richard Crawford. He determined that yearling females began nesting later, laid fewer eggs, and fledged fewer and slightly smaller young than did older females. Where yearling females were primary nesters on the territory (first to nest), they performed better.

A detailed study of growth rates and sex ratios of Redwing nestlings showed that males grow faster than females, attaining a greater weight. This permits the sexing of Redwing nestlings on the basis of weight by day eight. Even by day ten, however, there was still some overlap in weight of the two sexes.

Predation pressure on Redwing eggs and nestlings was the subject of a study by Frank Shipley in 1979. He found that predation pressure was related to water depth at nest sites, habitat type, and number of young in the nest. Predators were thought to be of three types: other bird species, large mammals, and small mammals. Mammalian pressure was greater for shallow-water nests than for deep-water nests. Large mammal predators were primarily raccoons, with some skunks and, to a lesser extent, mink.

10

Between Breeding Seasons

Molt

Invariably, one day in late July there is a black feather beneath the oaks in my yard. It is a wing feather from a Common Grackle and it tells me that summer is nearing an end. It is the first sign of molt, that process of shedding old feathers and growing new ones, a way of replacing worn plumage.

Redwings undergo a complete molt in late summer and fall, adult males assuming slightly greenish, glossy black feathers and bright new red shoulder patches. The most critical period of feather replacement occurs from late August through September. Owing to the fact that several wing or tail feathers are missing or incompletely renewed, some birds have a slower and labored flight. Tailless Redwings in flight have an odd appearance. The molt in most Redwings is nearly complete by the first week of October.

Brooke Meanley and Gormon Bond noted that fall migration to southern wintering grounds usually doesn't begin until the two outermost wing feathers and the two innermost or central tail feathers are two-thirds or more grown. This is substantiated by Richard Dolbeer who, analyzing about 11,000 recoveries of more than 700,000 Redwings banded between 1924–74, found that (among many other things) except in the Northwest, Redwings did not migrate long distances until after the fall molt was completed. Tailless Redwings flying in to fall roosts are probably local breeding birds. Thus, though some fall migrants may still be molting, there is a general correlation between replacement of wing and tail feathers and fall migration.

Male Redwings lose their dull, weathered feathers and gain new feathers, many of which are edged with brown. These brown edges, which are more pronounced in subadult males and also are found in females, largely disappear before spring as the result of wear and, especially, breakage. The nuptial plumage of many kinds of birds is attained through the breakage and loss of dull-colored feather tips and margins. The Snow Bunting, for example, goes from a brown and dull-white plumage over winter to its immaculate black and white spring colors. The male House Sparrow has a grayish breast in winter, but by spring it has a conspicuous black bib.

Young Redwings go through a complete postjuvenile molt, beginning in August, its onset depending on their age. The shoulder patches of young males are more orange than red (though we've already drawn attention to the range of plumage they bear, from femalelike to adult malelike plumages) with subterminal spots of black. It is the orange and black-spotted epaulets that distinguish first-year males (immatures) from adults, although by spring the younger birds also have less glossy black plumage.

Some variation in the color of epaulet feathers may be due to diet. The red and yellow pigments (carotenoids) found in birds have to be ingested with food. Hence, what a Redwing has been feeding on prior to molt and growth of new feathers likely affects its color. (During my graduate years I attempted to test this by plucking the feathers of captive birds..After plucking, the new feathers came in with less red. Colors diminished with repeated plucking. This suggested that the supply of carotenoid in the birds' bodies was gradually depleted.)

"The difference in the progress of molt of adults and young seems to be too slight to influence differential migration," Meanley reported in 1964.

Annual Cycle

The Redwing's annual cycle was divided into five seasonal periods by Dolbeer as follows: (1) the reproductive period—April 25 to July 31; (2) the postreproductive period—August 1 to October 15; (3) the period of fall migration—October 16 to December 9; (4) birds in winter roosts—December 10 to February 20; and (5) the spring migration-prereproductive period—February 21 to April 24. For a species as widely distributed as the Redwing, it isn't easy to define precise periods of activity, but these dates encompass the nesting and immediate postfledging period for most Redwings in North America. "Red-wings were sedentary in late summer in the Great Lakes and Midwest regions; however, in New England, Red-wings often moved 200-250 km from their nesting sites by August," according to Dolbeer.

To a certain extent, apart from the breeding season, male and female Redwings do not socialize (except for younger males in the company of females).

Flocking and Roosting

Redwings gather in flocks as soon as they leave the territories, females and young in one group, adult males in another, although some flocks may contain both sexes and all ages. They prefer to roost at night in cattails, often using breeding marshes for this purpose. Occasionally, these flocks begin to roost while territories are still active, flocking birds patiently waiting until dusk, then quietly dropping down among the frantic residents. The calls of territorial males, squeals of alarm

A flock of male Redwings in the fall. (Robert R. Taylor)

from females—all this was a familiar sound at Wingra Marsh every year. As the season progresses the flocks increase in size.

Roosting, as pointed out by Pat Weatherhead, is not unique to blackbirds. "By definition, it is only resting or sleeping, an activity engaged in by all birds. Nor is communal roosting, in which a number of individuals of the same . . . species return to the same site each night to roost a particularly remarkable phenomenon." Meanley notes that Redwings and other icterids form roosts during every month of the year, the low point, of course, being the breeding season. The largest numbers are reached in fall when the increment of young has been added to the population.

In fall, on more than one occasion near Madison, Wisconsin, I trudged through frozen beds of cattails long before dawn heading for the edge of a small lake where we hunted ducks. Often the Redwings roosting in the cattails were put to flight by my noisy passage, clattering up before me with a chorus of alarm notes, "chucks," squawks, and thrashing wings. Standing on the edge of the marsh, looking over the water, decoys barely discernible in the predawn hours, the fluttering sound of Redwings overhead heading for upland feeding grounds was a pleasant part of duck hunting.

Meanley and Bond estimated that late-summer roosts on the Patuxent River marshes in Maryland contained a peak population of two million birds. This coincided with the period of maximum food availability during late August and September. By the end of October, when almost all Redwings had completed their molt, the population was down to 100,000. Banding studies showed that this population was largely of local origin.

In the northern parts of their range, that is, southern Manitoba, Lawrie Smith and Ralph Bird report that small flocks of adult male Redwings return to the breeding grounds in late March to early April. Flocks of returning males increase greatly by the third week in April. Females first appear during the last week of April. The last flocks of either sex arrive by mid-May. Flocks break up when they reach the breeding ground. Later, family groups of females and young gradually join other flocks. Throughout July and August these larger flocks forage in the upland areas near their night roost, which is usually in a large marshy or shrubby area near water. This generally is the picture across the range of the species, although in more southerly areas birds reach the breeding ground sooner.

In the coastal states, of course, local resident birds flock together with migrants from the north. Manitoba birds forage daily in flocks at wintering sites mainly in Arkansas, Tennessee, and Texas. The wintering northern population begins to move northward in February.

Autumn flocks in Manitoba feed on cereal grains, weed seeds, and insects. The daily pattern of behavior is remarkably consistent. Beginning at sunrise, Redwings leave the night roosts and fly to nearby fields to feed. After feeding they fly to the nearest water to drink, then rest in trees near the watering spot, where they preen and sing sporadically. This cycle of movements seemed to be repeated throughout the day. About two hours before sunset, the birds begin returning to the night roost.

On the Patuxent River marshes, Redwings regularly fed on the flowers and especially on the seeds of wild rice, which grows in profusion in or near the roost. However, as soon as corn began to ripen in adjacent fields, birds turned to feeding on corn.

Flyways

One of the things ornithologists have learned from the recovery of banded birds is that there are definite routes that are followed as birds migrate from summer breeding grounds to wintering grounds. These routes vary greatly from species to species, but one concept formed nearly five decades ago is the "flyway." Flyways are large geographic areas of the continent through which large numbers of migrants pass.

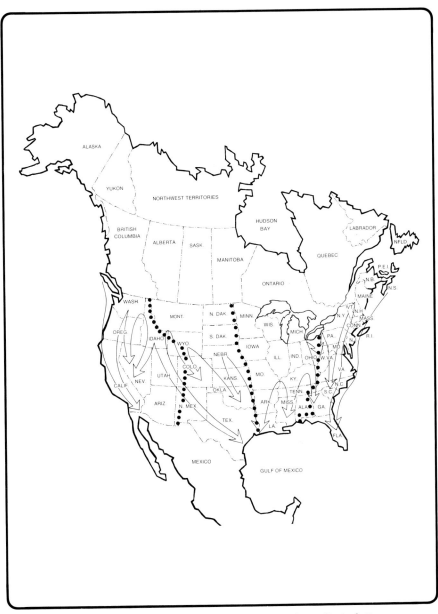

The major United States waterfowl flyways. (Courtesy Ducks Unlimited, Canada)

In the United States there are four major flyways (extending into Canada to a limited extent), from west to east: the Pacific Flyway, the Central Flyway, the Mississippi Flyway, and the Atlantic Flyway.

For waterfowl-management purposes the U.S. Fish and Wildlife Service arbitrarily set the United States flyway boundaries partly along state borders. The western limit of the Mississippi Flyway, for example, is almost a straight line along the western borders of Minnesota, Iowa, Missouri, Arkansas, and Louisiana. The eastern boundary is more irregular, running along the western borders of Pennsylvania, West Virginia, Virginia, North Carolina, Georgia, and Florida. Various species of waterfowl freely migrate across these lines, sometimes making long flights from west to east, but a large proportion of ducks and geese, and other species, do pass down (and up) the Mississippi Flyway, wintering in the Gulf Coast states of Louisiana, Mississippi, and Alabama.

Redwings using the Mississippi Flyway come from a broader northern zone, from Saskatchewan and North Dakota on the west, and from western Ontario and Ohio on the east. This is the largest Redwing flyway in the country, according to Brooke Meanley. Some Redwings winter as far north as Colorado and western Nebraska, but the majority migrate to wintering grounds from Missouri, Kentucky, and Virginia southward.

Flocks of blackbirds congregate in fall before their migration south in northeastern and north-central Canada. Sixty-six roosts in a study area in Quebec in fall 1977 contained an estimated 500,000 blackbirds. Of these, Redwings comprised 77 percent in fall and 74 percent in spring. The same sites were used in both spring and fall. Since fall counts were made before September, it was believed that these were local breeding birds. It takes several weeks for birds from the north to reach southern wintering grounds. Birds from large areas fly to traditional roosting sites where they have access to various sources and kinds of food throughout the winter period. There are advantages and disadvantages to roosting in large numbers.

"By concentrating into dense roosting aggregations of up to several million birds, blackbird and Starling populations are vulnerable to large-scale die offs caused by disease, . . . severe local weather conditions, . . . or man-induced stress. . .,"according to Dolbeer.

The greatest concentrations of Redwings in the southern states, as noted by Meanley, occur in the Coastal Plain Province (Atlantic Flyway) in or near grain-producing areas, in the commercial rice belts and river deltas of Arkansas, Louisiana, and Mississippi, and in the Gulf coastal marshes. Large numbers occur in the Virginia-Carolina peanut belt, in the south Atlantic coastal marshes, and in the lower Florida peninsula. The Texas coastal rice belt and the great valley of California are other important concentration areas.

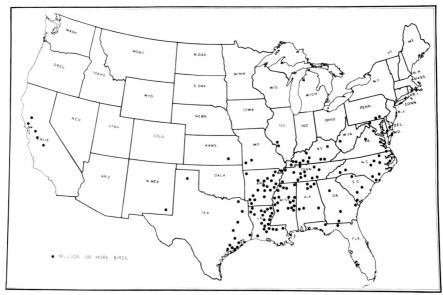

The major wintering blackbird/starling roosts, 1960–65. (Meanley 1971)

Winter Roosts

On the wintering grounds, roosts are formed that vary in size from a handful of birds to several million. Redwings and other blackbirds (plus the ubiquitous and exotic starlings) roost in large concentrations mainly in the southeastern United States. Several different populations and geographic races may be represented in a roosting population. "The winter concentration of blackbirds and starlings in the lower Mississippi Valley is the largest found in any section of the United States at any season. Based on the estimated number of birds that occupy roosts located in Arkansas, Louisiana, Mississippi, and Tennessee, 200 million blackbirds and starlings are calculated to winter in the region. . . . Most of the birds wintering in the central areas of Kentucky, Tennessee, and Alabama come from the Great Lakes region. . . . There are approximately 150 major winter roosts, each containing a million or more blackbirds and starlings. Some roosts have been known to contain from 20 to 30 million birds," Meanley writes.

During the winter-roost period, breeding populations from widely divergent areas occur in individual roosts. In the Gulf Coastal states and other southern areas, permanent resident Redwings (and Boat-tailed Grackles) intermingle with their northern cohorts. In general, for the period 1966–76, blackbird and starling populations were shown to be increasing across much of North America. This accounts for some reports of increased roosting populations. From 1966–69 to 1977–80, Redwings in the Mississippi River valley area showed an increase of 51 percent.

Winter surveys of roosts in the southeastern United States have been conducted annually with the cooperation of hundreds of birders who make estimates and fill out forms for the U.S. Fish and Wildlife Service. The winter inventory of 1974–75 revealed the presence of more than 110 million Redwings in the eastern states, more than 78 million in the western states, and a total United States population of 189,524,000, as noted in chapter 1. The combined Redwing-icterid-starling population in the United States is estimated to be 400 million. "Three-fourths of the total U.S. blackbird-starling population is found in the relatively humid East; the comparatively arid West lacks the food, cover, and water to support a larger proportion of the population," Meanley states.

It is the sociability of the blackbird that results in concentrations of large numbers in autumn and winter. Alexander Wilson, the ornithologist who competed with Audubon, (and who is commemorated in the Wilson Ornithological Society), remarked in 1832 on the phenomenon: "Sometimes they appeared driving about like an enormous black cloud carried before the wind, varying its shape every moment; sometimes suddenly rising from the fields around me with a noise like thunder; while the glittering of innumerable wings of the brightest vermillion amid the black cloud they formed, produced on these occasions a very striking and splendid effect."

T. Gilbert Pearson writes with equal admiration of their flocking behavior:

At this time they may be seen in flocks numbering tens of thousands, and they present a marvelous spectacle as they fly with all the precision of perfectly trained soldiers. I have seen fully thirty thousand of them while in full flight suddenly turn to the right or left or at the same instant swoop downward as if they were all driven by common impulse. They perform very wonderful feats of flight when on the wing. Sometimes a long billow of moving birds will pass across the fields, the ends of the flying regiment alternately sinking and rising, or even appearing to tumble about like a sheet of paper in a high wind.

Weatherhead calls attention to the enjoyment of watching the fall gathering of blackbirds in roosts. At the conclusion of a popular account of the damage they inflict on crops, and studies underway to control their numbers, he writes:

I began by saying that in spite of becoming a common phenomenon, blackbird roosts were unfamiliar to most people. It is therefore appropriate that I finish by providing some clues to locating them. Keep your eyes open for flocks of birds in flight an hour or so before sunset. You may find that half the fun is in the chase. If you lose sight of the original flock, simply stop your car and wait. If the roost is of any size at all another flock should come by heading in the same direction. With luck it will take only a few such flocks to lead you to the spot. If you happen upon a fairly large roost it would be worth your while to return the following evening and view the performance in its entirety. You may be surprised to find that even birds as common as blackbirds can provide you with an uncommon and rewarding experience.

11

A Plethora of Blackbirds

When male Red-winged Blackbirds reach their northern breeding grounds in early spring, the marsh is often cold and snowbound, and food is noticeably scarce. Consequently, the territorial males spend much of their time away from the marsh foraging for food. Occasionally, however, Redwings may be seen industriously pecking at cattail heads; this has led at least one observer to report cattail seeds as a food item for this species. These seeds, however, are minute and it is doubtful that any are eaten. Numerous observations have convinced me that Redwings do, however, prey upon the larvae of the Cattail Moth (*Lymnaceia phragmitella*), which regularly overwinter in cattail heads.

These small larvae, about half an inch in length, occur in abundance and may be found by carefully breaking open cattail heads. Usually the larvae are found close along the central stalk, where they feed on the seeds. The cattail down is kept from blowing away, once it has been freed by their feeding activities, by the abundance of silk the larvae spin, thereby tying the down together. In the process of searching for these concentrated bits of protein, Redwings loosen the down. I have vivid recollections of more than one bird with cattail down momentarily clinging to its bill and head. It is the feeding activities of the Redwing that serve, in part, to bring about the characteristic puffing out of portions of cattail heads as spring advances.

It is a long way from that pleasant scene on a marsh with a few Redwings foraging for natural prey to the image of Redwings as creatures capable of massive agricultural damage, descending in immense flocks on corn and other crops. Unfortunately, Redwings are one of the major agricultural pests and nuisance birds over much of the eastern and central United States, California, and southern Canada. In late summer and autumn, especially near marshes, they feed on ripening corn, green oats, barley, flax, sunflowers, rice, and other crops. Most crop damage in late summer is caused by locally breeding or locally produced birds.

Imagine hundreds of acres of standing corn with the cobs nearly husked and grainless, all the result of heavy foraging by Redwings and grackles. What a job they do! In their search for food to nourish themselves they can literally strip a field bare, returning from their nocturnal roosts to spend successive days in the fields, feasting on man's hard-earned produce. No wonder farmers and agriculturists look upon their wheeling flocks with such dismay.

In 1832 Nuttall noted:

About the beginning of September these flocks, by their formidable numbers, do great damage to the unripe corn, which is now a favorite repast; and they are sometimes seen whirling and driving over the devoted cornfields and meadows so as to darken the sky with their numbers. The destruction at this time made among them by the gun and the Hawks [sic] produces but little effect upon the remainder who continue fearlessly, and in spite of all opposition, from morning to night to ravage the cornfields while anything almost remains to be eaten. . . . When the reeds become dry, advantage is taken of the circumstance to destroy these unfortunate gormandizers [sic] by fire; and those who might escape the flames are shot down in vast numbers as they hover and scream around the spreading conflagration.

Note the date; a bushel of corn must have meant a lot in those days. Incidentally, the fire technique has been used in modern times. Today it would be strongly opposed by naturalists, conservationists, and the general public.

Audubon commented on the management aspect of Redwings as follows:

The havock [sic] made amongst them is scarcely credible. I have heard that upwards of fifty have been killed at a shot, and am the more inclined to believe such accounts that I have myself shot hundreds in the course of an afternoon, killing from ten to fifteen with each discharge.

From Colonial times in New England, Redwings and particularly grackles, were known as crop pests. Colonists there, for example,

found it necessary to levy a fine unless a landowner killed a certain number of "blackbirds" annually. Crop-destroying "blackbirds" include particularly the Common Grackle, but the Brewer's Blackbird, Rusty Blackbird, Yellow-headed Blackbird, Brown-headed Cowbird, and Bobolink are also offenders. The exotic Common Starling (not a member of the blackbird family) soon became widespread and now accounts for many numbers in large roosts.

Because all these birds are insectivorous for the main part of the year, devouring insects and other invertebrates, many of which are harmful to crops, there is a dilemma. Agricultural authorities and wildlife biologists, seeking ways to curb crop losses, see blackbirds as serious pests, but also recognize their beneficial role as insectivorous birds.

In 1900 Foster E. A. Beal, of the U.S. Biological Survey, examined more than a thousand stomachs of Redwings to ascertain their food habits, using specimens collected at various times of the year. He and a number of other arduous workers concluded that although the Redwing was a pest at certain times, generally they must be considered beneficial. By and large, Redwings feed on insects and other invertebrate animals during the breeding season, but in fall and winter they turn to seeds, including a variety of crops.

Arthur Allen, after looking over the available data in the literature, decided to investigate the food habits of birds in his New York marsh study area, collecting and analyzing the stomachs of more than a hundred birds over a three-year period. He was able to show how changes in diet could be related to the life cycle of the bird and environmental changes in the marsh. During the early breeding season lepidopterous (moth)larvae prevailed; thereafter, dipterous (fly) larvae were most often taken. He noted that after the Redwings left the marsh for the uplands, before fall migration, their diet changed radically from insects to seeds. He found a corresponding change in the size of the gizzard; because of the switch from soft-bodied prey to seeds, the gizzard increases in size and musculature to accommodate the greater effort required to grind seeds.

A corresponding change in the shape of the bill was noted by John Davis; presumably through wear and tear, from a fairly long, pointed bill to manipulate insect prey, the Redwing's bill becomes shorter and shorter to handle hard seeds. Ralph Bird and Lawrie Smith found that when insect food increased in the diet of Redwings, "mineral grit decreased, its function evidently being carried out by the hard parts of insects." The jaws and chitinous plate found on each side of the knee of the hind leg of grasshoppers in particular were retained—"one gizzard contained 44 jaws and 77 chitinous plates."

In California, Pablo Soriano pointed out that

Economically, in the widest human interests, the Brewer and red-winged black-bird are beneficial, being more insectivorous than vegetarian in food habits. However, being gregarious birds . . . now and then they inflict such great damage on crops that to give them full protection is not fair to the farmer whose crops are immediately threatened. It is wisest, then, that these birds be protected during the breeding season when they destroy many insect pests, and that the farmers and growers allow them to nest on their farms. But when and where they become vegetarian and inflict real damage to crops, then their numbers should be reduced, though only to such degree that the damage by those remaining can hardly be felt.
[It seems illogical to protect a species for part of the year and then kill it at another.]

Others in that period voiced different concerns. An unidentified "R.E." in 1936 wrote some purple prose protesting the refusal of the U.S. Biological Survey to grant protection to the Rusty Blackbird and Red-winged Blackbird, citing reports proving these species to be insectivorous and beneficial.

The refusal to stop a "shoot" of blackbirds, organized to satisfy the sadism of gunners, is a warning that no birds in the United States can be considered protected while the ammunition companies spread propaganda against our wild creatures in order to induce the public to buy shells and guns. The Biological Survey itself sets such a deplorable example of slaughter of both birds and mammals in its wholesale poisoning operations. Readers of the Condor and the E.C.C. pamphlet, "Its alive! Kill it!!" will recall to what depths of cruelty the Biological Survey sank in the poisoning of the Redwinged Blackbirds in California in 1931.

This strong-minded point of view is not likely to meet with the approval of administrators and others faced with the real problem of too many blackbirds in croplands. Incidentally, Redwings and other blackbirds have been protected in the United States since 1918 under the Federal Migratory Bird Treaty Act. An amendment to the act, however, permits farmers to destroy blackbirds that are in the act of damaging or about to damage crops. Blackbirds (excluding orioles, meadowlarks, and bobolinks) remain unprotected in Canada.

From California to the New England states and southern Canada, the problem of crop depredation by various species of blackbirds and Starlings has greatly increased. This is partly owing to a vast increase in acreage of susceptible crops over the past several decades and to an increase in birds. Recent expansion of corn acreage in southern Quebec has resulted in an increasing Redwing population. Redwings, in particular, are highly adaptable and from early days on, nested in man-made habitat where marshes were not available, using hayfields as readily as if they had always occupied uplands. Thus, as more hay meadows developed, Redwings found new homes. In the midwestern

United States, for example, most Redwings now nest in upland habitat.

"The clearing of woodland for hay and pasture has provided habitat similar enough to marshes that the birds [Redwings] have successfully expanded their choice of nest-sites. . . . these agricultural areas are now responsible for the majority of the species' productivity. If farmers took their first hay off before any young could have been produced, approximately the end of May (southern Quebec and eastern Ontario), it might be possible to lower productivity," Weatherhead and Bider wrote in 1979.

Ohio recently changed its practice of cultivating alfalfa. "This reduced the nesting habitat of the Red-winged Blackbird and cut out a year class for at least 10 years; in other words one year of each of three has failed because alfalfa was planted with winter wheat and was not suitable for nesting red-wings the first year," according to Maurice Giltz in a letter written to me in 1982.

Twenty-four states, which accounted for 98 percent of the total acreage harvested, were surveyed for damage to ripening corn in 1970. The estimated mean loss to birds amounted to more than $9,300,000. Of these twenty-four states, New York showed the highest average loss to birds, and Red-winged Blackbirds were responsible for most of the observed damage. In Ontario, where the Redwing is the primary depredator, the 1977 loss of field corn was estimated at 43,120 tons or a .7 percent reduction in overall yield. Mel Dyer reports that Redwing depredation does not always result in loss of corn, because feeding on the tips of the ears may stimulate extra growth, but this has since been disproved.

In Arkansas and Louisiana, Redwings are found near rice fields during much of the year. They are primarily rice feeders (nearly 54 percent of their diet), but they feed largely on waste grain. Brooke Meanley reported in 1971 that Redwings on the Grande Prairie of eastern Arkansas and the coastal prairie of Louisiana and Texas had 13 percent rice in their diet; otherwise the birds fed on weed seeds and injurious insects.

Four species of icterids were found to be responsible for most of the damage to rice crops: the Redwing, the Brown-headed Cowbird, the Common Grackle, and the Boat-tailed Grackle. Local populations were believed to be the cause of the majority of the damage. Some five million acres of marshland—prime breeding grounds for Redwings and Boat-tailed Grackles—are found on the coastal prairie of Louisiana and Texas. Rice has been an important crop in the region since 1900. Cultivation of rice has spread to other sections of Arkansas, Louisiana, Mississippi, Tennessee, and Missouri. "In effect," says Meanley, "man has taken rice to the blackbirds." Reports of increased depredation on sprouting and ripening rice in the southern United States is perhaps due to relatively large increases of Redwings and Common Grackles. Arthur Bent notes that "Several observers have mentioned the great service that marsh hawks perform in the southern ricefields by driving away Bobolinks and blackbirds more effectively than hired men with guns, thus saving considerable expense."

Redwings were the only species associated with harvested soybean fields near a major winter roost in Tennessee in 1975–76. "A primary food source in these fields appeared to be cocklebur, a common weed in soybeans. . . .Red-wings probably had the least impact on agriculture of all roosting species," according to a 1978 study by Dolbeer and colleagues.

Cocklebur seeds were judged to be an important food item for Redwings at sites in North Carolina, South Carolina, Georgia, and Alabama. "The manner of extracting the seed from the seemingly tough, prickly hull was observed at Montgomery," Meanley writes. "A bird would pick up a bur from the ground in an old cornfield, fly to the limb of a tree along the border of the field, place the nut on the limb between its feet, and hack at the husk until the seed was exposed."

In southeastern Virginia in late October the diet of Redwings consists of peanuts and corn, supplemented by various native plant foods. According to Meanley, "Peanuts were much more important in the diet than would have been expected from the records in the literature. Peanut shells dropped by blackbirds have been found in the Dismal Swamp more than a mile from the nearest peanut field."

Estimates of Loss

The annual overall loss from "blackbird" damage to farm crops in southern Manitoba has been estimated at two million dollars. Blackbird damage in North Dakota, South Dakota and Minnesota now is about 12 million dollars and the United States total is given as 50 million dollars annually. In many areas "blackbirds" are the chief agricultural pest and many thousands of dollars have been spent annually in an attempt to learn more about these birds and to devise methods to reduce their numbers and to reduce crop depredation. The major loss by far is to corn and the major pest is the Redwing.

"Bird damage to corn and small grain crops in southern Quebec and eastern Ontario is due in large part to Red-winged Blackbirds," Weatherhead and Bider report. "This species has been increasing in this area, with the breeding-season population estimated to be between 4 and 5 million birds."

In a 1978 article in *Bird-Banding*, Dolbeer wrote: "Red-winged Blackbirds are sometimes rather serious depredators of maturing grain crops (especially corn) in certain areas of North America during August and September. . . . The analyses on movements between the reproductive period and post-reproductive period based on about 11,000 recoveries accumulated from the banding of over 700,000 Redwings suggest that most of these depredation problems are caused by locally (within 200 km) breeding or produced birds and not by far-ranging migrants.

The results of the first nationwide survey of bird damage to corn (1970) were published in the "Conservation Section" of the *Wilson Bulletin*, a major bird journal. The total direct loss to birds (several kinds) was estimated to be over six million bushels.

Apart from the problems of crop depredation, wildlife staff at federal, state, and provincial levels are faced with a grim task, that of reducing over-abundant Redwing populations. The problem is that Redwings (and other icterids, as well as starlings) are so highly sociable, flocking and roosting in extremely high numbers. "Blackbirds" have used such roosts for hundreds of years, but in recent times urban sprawl has brought roost sites into proximity with residential areas. The result—a lot of complaints: too much noise, too strong an odor, and the possibility of birds in large numbers spreading disease (histoplasmosis).

Control Methods

Some of these winter roosts are huge. At Greenbrier, Tennessee, for example, there was a single roost holding an estimated 23 million birds! Control measures in the past have included shooting (not very effective), dynamiting roosts, floodlights, noise-makers of various types, chemical repellants, poisons, detergent spray followed by cold water, and removal of some of the trees in the roost site (the latter method being fairly successful). Naturally, a large segment of the public objects to seeing birds treated inhumanely, but the magnitude of the problem has brought the issue to the courts.

Appeals to the federal Environmental Protection Agency (EPA) were made to eradicate nine large roosts in western Kentucky and Tennessee. EPA and the courts gave their approval, whereupon several environmentalist groups sought a court injunction to halt the operations. In the end, EPA and the courts approved the plans and operations were mounted against five roosts, ranging in size from 400,000 to 3,000,000 birds. Helicopters were used to spray the birds with detergent to make their plumage more wettable, and then the birds were drenched with cold water. Consequently, many died from being chilled. The total kill in the five operations accounted for an estimated four million birds.

That's an incredible number, but only in a relative sense. Some perspective on bird control may be gained by noting that in South Africa 112 million crop-destroying Red-billed Weaverbirds were killed in 1966–67. Ken Garner, of the U.S. Fish and Wildlife Service, estimated that upward of 77 million blackbirds occupy 59 known winter roosts in the Kentucky-Tennessee area, and a further 54 roosts in adjoining Arkansas contained another 40 million. John Webb and Brooke Meanley, also of the U.S. Fish and Wildlife Service, estimated in a 1969–70 report that there were 350 million "blackbirds" in 674 major known roosts. Meanley has provided an excellent report on the roosting habits of Redwings in the southern United States: on one large roost in deciduous thickets on the Arkansas Grande Prairie, Redwings were crowded along branches at an average of about three birds per foot. In some cases branches were broken by the weight of the birds.

As yet, despite scattered control operations, there has been no reported decline of any size in the several species found at these winter roosts. What with that many birds this should be no surprise. All blackbirds have a high reproductive capacity and probably large winter kills can be absorbed by the several species involved. Dolbeer concluded that "reduction of populations of Redwings that cause localized late-summer agricultural damage probably cannot be practically achieved through the mass killing of blackbirds in a few winter roosts in the southern United States . . . [and] the large scale reduction of Red-wing numbers at a few winter roosts probably will not result in any large-scale reduction of specific local breeding populations of Red-wings in North America the following summer. . . . " High mortality at a single roost or cluster of roosts would be spread among Redwings over a wide breeding area.

The effect of surfactant (detergent) spraying of Redwings in spring roosts is reported by Weatherhead and colleagues to have had some potential for reducing crop damage in Quebec. "This potential is proximately limited by the small number of spring roosts with sufficient birds, the short duration of maximum roost occupancy, the use of some roosts by protected species later in the spring, and the limited occurrence of precipitation to make the surfactant effective in killing birds. Since males would be affected to a far greater extent than females, the feasibility may be ultimately limited by the ability of the surplus males in the population to replace those males killed."

Large-scale "extermination" of blackbirds at winter roosts was examined by five biologists at Queen's University, Ontario, who concluded: "Species composition of the Fort Campbell, Kentucky 1974–75 flock was found to be dynamic both in size and relative abundance of species. . . . Stomach analyses revealed that in addition to the consumption of some economically important grain, blackbirds were feeding on weed seeds and insect pests such as army worms and corn borers."

In September 1981 I visited two major roost sites in the Portage la Prairie, Manitoba, area, where farmers are planting an increasing acreage to corn and sunflowers. Because the Portage district is within a few miles of the famed Delta Marsh and the Assiniboine River, thousands of Redwings that roost nearby in late summer and autumn are attracted to this prime source of food. The two most popular overnight roosts for the feeding Redwings are a cattail marsh, formed through development of a highway cloverleaf, and a much larger marsh on the Assiniboine River (resulting from a dam and water-diversion system), which is occupied by an estimated 100,000 blackbirds.

In the Portage area alone, an estimated annual crop loss worth $250,000 is expected. Although more than one species of "blackbird" is involved, the Redwing has been identified as the major culprit. When I had met with farmers there in 1978 to talk about the blackbird problem, there were some high tempers and strong recommendations. Some wanted to burn or even drain Delta Marsh; poison all the birds; or shoot them all. One can sympathize with the farmers' plight, but this kind of action is unacceptable to most citizens and does not really solve the problem. Similar drastic solutions (and worse) have been sought elsewhere, wherever blackbird depredation is a problem.

Recently, farmers in the Portage area formed the Central Plains Special Crops Protection Association, to reduce damage to crops by blackbirds. Funded by a Federal-Provincial grant for five years, the project is managed by Harry A. G. Harris, an energetic young biologist from Scotland, who gave me a firsthand look at control methods. Harris and his assistant are constantly on the run, operating a number of blackbird-scaring devices. Automatic propane "bangers," small cannon that can be timed to fire at given intervals, were thumping here and there like distant guns as we drove around the fields. Harry showed us special noisemakers, one that broadcast Redwing distress calls, another designed to produce a loud, weird sound. These latter operate on the principal that the noise drowns out the natural sound of blackbird voices, causing them to leave for fields with better acoustical effects.

The blackbirds we saw seemed to ignore both kinds of machines. They were somehow determined to forage in that particular field, and Harry admitted that no amount of shooting with shotguns and pistols that fire projectiles that make a great bang at a considerable distance, or anything else, seemed to deter this particular flock. As a result, the crop sustained a considerable loss.

Harry had tried several other devices that had been used elsewhere, such as large decoy live traps to capture birds that later can be destroyed; a peculiar device that fired a ring that flashed up a long metal pole before sliding back down again; a shieldlike affair that turned in the wind, flashing bright colors and acting as a scarecrow; and even a hawk-shaped kite suspended from a helium balloon! Decoy live traps, incidentally, have been found to be ineffective; they are expensive and the birds least likely to cause crop damage are the ones captured.

For some time one of the most effective blackbird-control techniques was the use of cracked corn coated with Avitrol. Blackbirds (and other species) eating the poisoned grain give off distress calls that frighten away the flock. In their study on the control of plant pests, Charles Stone and Glenn Hood write:

Use of Avitrol in a corn-growing area of 8 to 508 square miles in South Dakota over a 7-year period resulted in an 80% decline in Red-winged Blackbirds roosting in the area and a damage decline of over 90%. Although direct cause and effect cannot be proven, blackbird migration routes may have been changed through continual use and effects of the chemical. Avitrol and methiocarb (a contact repellant widely used to prevent damage by blackbirds) are two of the most promising agents for the alleviation of bird damage in agricultural crops and should prove very useful in many damage situations throughout the world.

In 1975, 7,293 acres of field corn in Ohio and 3,975 acres in Michigan were treated with Avitrol to control blackbird damage. However, Avitrol has not proved as effective as it originally was thought to be, and there has been a dramatic decrease in its use by Ohio farmers. The reasons for this are related to a substantial decline in the Redwing population in Ohio during the 1970s, as well as to a variety of problems that surfaced concerning Avitrol use, such as bait removal by crickets and a greater scrutiny by the farmer of the costs of Avitrol as compared to the benefits. "Many farmers are beginning to realize," Dolbeer wrote me in 1982, "that the actual cost in yield to an entire field caused by blackbirds is often not as great as might be suggested by a superficial visual survey of damage to selected parts of the field."

Experience in the Portage region suggests that no single technique alone is enough; a combination of several devices and, especially, continually shooting at flocks at odd moments, serves to drive them away or at least reduce the amount of damage. Often, it is simply a matter of moving birds from one field to another, but occasionally Redwings choose one field and feed in it constantly, doing an incredible amount of damage. Near Winnipeg, a market gardener suffered a complete loss from his seven-acre sweet-corn field. The total loss was estimated at ten thousand dollars, a big bill for one man.

Several times over the last decade a specialist with the Manitoba Department of Agriculture has sought to develop a means of marketing blackbird carcasses as a gourmet food in Japan. The Manitoba

Wildlife Branch has been approached several times—there is a file on the subject—but nothing has ever developed. The high labor cost involved in plucking and eviscerating birds is a factor impeding the proposal, but it would be one way of making use of birds now being trapped, killed, and discarded (in many areas besides Manitoba).

This is not the first use of blackbirds for food; Audubon wrote that "many are eaten and thought good by the country people, who make pot-pies of them." "Four and twenty blackbirds" had good meaning as late as the thirties. Johnson A. Neff notes that "Heerman wrote in 1853 of the large numbers of Tri-colored Red-wings shot for the market. This practice still continues, and during the past 5 years it is probable that fully 300,000 blackbirds of the combined red-winged group have been marketed from the Sacramento Valley, with no apparent change in the status of any of the birds involved. During the winter of 1935–36, 88,000 blackbirds were shipped from Biggs alone. . . . "

Richard Dolbeer, working in Ohio, where Redwings are especially abundant (an estimated eight million are found in Ohio during the nesting season), has concluded that direct reduction of blackbird populations is an unwise control method. He writes:

Successful programs to reduce damage must use one or more of a series of management measures, integrated with normal farming practices. The selection of management measures should be based on assessments of amount and type of bird damage likely to occur in a [corn] field and constraints imposed by farming practices. Management recommendations include (1) planting of hybrids with ear tips well covered by husks; (2) reduction of weed and insect populations to make the field less attractive to birds; (3) judicious use of mechanical frightening devices or a chemical frightening agent at the time the birds initially damage the maturing corn; (4) the provision of natural or planted food and cover sites outside the corn; and (5) harvesting the crop, especially sweet corn, as early as possible.

In 1981, according to Jerome Besser, there were twenty-five full-time employees of the U.S. Fish and Wildlife Service specifically dealing with the problems of blackbirds. Through coordination of state and federal research activities and projects, through imaginative research, and practical efforts aimed at reducing crop damage and blackbirds, these people are steadily progressing toward a better understanding of the problems and their solutions.

Somewhere in my files I have a clipping from *LIFE* magazine from many years ago showing a full-page photo of about a dozen adult male Redwings trapped by freezing spray on the edge of open water on one of the Great Lakes. The birds had probably been foraging along the ice when they became frozen to its surface and then engulfed. Only their heads and sharp bills showed above the shiny, translucent globules of ice in which each was trapped alive. There was no sign of alarm in their eyes. State conservation officials were shown in other photos carefully chopping loose the ice-encased birds and then thawing them out under a car heater, prior to releasing them. The Redwings in their balls of ice made a dramatic sight and one had to admire the tender care with which they were being rescued.

Wildlife officials at all levels are confronted, as we have seen, with problems of blackbird crop depredation and winter roosts of millions of birds. Still, I like to think of that picture of the men freeing the ice-trapped Redwings as a good example of the crucial relationship between man and nature.

Notes

References are listed in the Bibliography. When a reference is to one of several works by the same author, the particular citation is located below by page number and is identified, when necessary, by a phrase from the text.

29 A subspecies in Utah . . .: Behle 1940.

34 Courtship feeding has been reported . . . for the Yellow-headed Blackbird: Roberts 1909; the Rusty Blackbird: Kennard 1920; the Northern Oriole: Brackbill 1941; the Melodious Blackbird: Kendeigh 1952; the Brewer's Blackbird: Williams 1952.

36 An interesting array of homologous displays: Nero 1964; Orians and Christman 1968.

51 Orians and Christman 1968.

51 . . . they sing many renditions of a single song type: Smith and Reid 1979; Yasukawa 1981.

51 . . . song functions primarily in territory defense: Yasukawa 1981.

51 . . . but some experimentally muted males: Smith 1976.

52 . . . the trill functions in species recognition: Beletsky et al. 1980.

52 . . . it also has been shown to influence female recruitment: Weatherhead and Robertson 1977a; Yasukawa 1981.

53 Orians 1960.

56 Orians and Christman 1968.

61 . . . near perfect female mimics; Selander and Giller 1960.

61 Smith 1972a.

66 Orians 1961.

66 Peek 1971.

66 This would explain the attempted territoriality: Yasukawa 1979.

71 Nice 1943.

73 Searcy 1979a.

76 Polygyny . . . has been recorded: Allen 1914; Roberts 1932; Linsdale 1938; Mayr 1941.

76 . . . a few observers have reported this species to be monogamous: Williams 1940; McIlhenny 1937.

76 Orians 1980.

77 Female Redwings experimentally induced: Knos and Stickley 1974.

77 Holcomb 1974.

77 Howard 1971.

78 In the Redwing, the pairing bond: Williams 1952.

78 Meanley 1965.

81 Nice 1943.

84 Nice 1950.

88 Sexual chases in the Brewer's Blackbird: Williams 1952.

92 Howard 1929.

93	Nice 1943.
97	The precopulatory behavior of both male and female Brewer's Blackbird: Williams 1952.
97–98	Similar behavior has also been noted in the Tricolored Redwing: Lack and Emlen 1939; Orians and Christman 1968; the Yellow-headed Blackbird: Ammann 1938; and several other icterids: Nero 1964.
98	. . . similar in the Snow Bunting: Tinbergen 1939.
98	Howard 1929.
98	Nice 1943.
98	Ingeniously designed experiments in Colorado: Bray et al. 1975.
98	A later study along the same lines: Roberts and Kennelly 1980.
104	Francis 1973a; 1971.
105	Holcomb 1968.
106	Orians 1980.
115	Peek et al. 1972.
115	Holcomb 1979.
121	Nice 1937.
121	. . . suggestive of the behavior of fledglings begging for food: See Nice 1943.
122	Even by day ten, however: Holcomb and Twiest 1970.
123	Dolbeer 1978.
124	Dolbeer 1978.
124	Dolbeer 1982.
125	Weatherhead 1981.
128	Meanley 1971.
128	Some Redwings winter as far north as Colorado: Dolbeer, 1980.
128	Flocks of blackbirds congregate: Robertson et al. 1978.
128	Since fall counts were made before September: Weatherhead et al. 1980.
128	"By concentrating into dense roosting aggregations": Dolbeer 1982.
128	Meanley 1965.
128	The Texas coastal rice belt: Meanley 1975.
129	Several different populations: Meanley 1965.
129	Meanley 1975.
130	This accounts for some reports of increased roosting populations: Dolbeer and Stehn 1979.
130	From 1966–69 to 1977–80, Redwings: Johnson et al. 1982.
130	Winter surveys of roosts: Webb and Meanley 1973.
130	Meanley 1975.
130	Wilson quoted in Bent 1958.
130	Pearson quoted in Bent 1958.
130	Weatherhead 1981.
132	Most crop damage in late summer: Dolbeer 1978.
136	The estimated mean loss to birds: Stone et al. 1972.
136	Red-winged Blackbirds were responsible for most of the observed damage: Stone et al. 1973.
136	. . . the 1977 loss of field corn was estimated at 43,120 tons: Tyler and Kannenbert 1980.

136	. . . but this has since been disproved: Worenecki et al. 1980.
136	. . . they feed largely on waste grain: Edwin R. Kalmbach in Meanley 1971.
136	Reports of increased depredation: Johnson et al. 1982.
137	Meanley 1962.
137	. . . damage to farm crops in southern Manitoba: Harris, pers. comm. 1981.
137	Blackbird damage . . . is given as 50 million dollars annually: Jerome E. Besser, pers. comm. 1981.
137	Weatherhead and Bider 1979.
138	The results of the first nationwide survey of bird damage: Stone et al. 1972.
138	The total kill . . . an estimated four million birds: Rivinus 1976.
139	. . . 112 million crop-destroying Red-billed Weaverbirds . . . were killed in 1966–67: Stone and Hood 1979.
139	Meanley 1965.
139	Dolbeer 1978.
139	Species composition of the Fort Campbell, Kentucky, 1974–75 flock: Robertson et al. 1978.
142	Dolbeer 1980.

Bibliography

Allen, Arthur A. 1914. The Red-winged Blackbird: a study in the ecology of a cat-tail marsh. *Proceedings Linnaean Society New York* 24–25: 43–128.

American Ornithologists' Union. 1957. *Check-list of North American Birds.* 5th ed. Baltimore.

A. O. U. 1982. Thirty-fourth supplement to the check-list of North American birds. Supplement to *AUK* 99.

Ammann, George A. The life history and distribution of the Yellow-headed Blackbird. 1938. Ph.D. diss. Univ. Michigan Library, Ann Arbor.

Andrew, Richard J. 1961. The displays given by passerines in courtship and reproductive fighting: A review. *Ibis* 103a:315–48, 549–79.

Audubon, John J. 1834. *Ornithological biography.* Edinburgh: Adam Black.

Austin, Oliver L. 1971. *Families of birds.* New York: Golden Press.

Baird, Spencer F., Thomas M. Brewer, and Robert Ridgway. 1874. *A history of North American birds: Land birds.* Vol. 2.

Beal, Foster E.L. 1900. Food of the bobolink, blackbirds, and grackles. *United States Department of Agriculture, Division of Biological Survey Bulletin* 13:22–30.

Beecher, William J. 1942. *Nesting birds and the vegetation substrate.* Chicago: Chicago Ornithological Society.

———. 1950. Convergent evolution in the American orioles. *Wilson Bulletin* 62:51–86.

Beer, James R. 1950. The reproductive cycle of the muskrat in Wisconsin. *Journal of Wildlife Management* 14:151–56.

Beer, James R., and Douglas Tibbitts. 1950. Nesting behavior of the Red-wing Blackbird. *The Flicker* 22:61–77.

Behle, William H. 1940. Distribution and characters of the Utah Red-wing. *Wilson Bulletin* 52:234–40.

Beletsky, L. David, Stella Chao, and Douglas G. Smith. 1980. An investigation of song-based species recognition in the Red-winged Blackbird (*Agelaius phoeniceus*). *Behaviour* 73:189–203.

Bent, Arthur C. 1937. Life histories of North American birds of prey. *United States National Museum Bulletin* 170. Dover reprint, 1961.

———. 1958. Life histories of North American blackbirds, orioles, tanagers, and allies. Dover reprint, 1965.

———. 1948. Life histories of North American nuthatches, wrens, thrashers and their allies. *United States National Museum Bulletin* 195: 1–475.

Bird, Ralph D., and Lawrie B. Smith. 1964. The food habits of the Red-winged Blackbird, *Agelaius phoeniceus*, in Manitoba. *Canadian Field-Naturalist* 78:179–86.

Brackbill, Hervey. 1941. Additional cases of 'courtship feeding.' *Auk* 58:57.

Bray, Olin, James J. Kennedy, and Joseph L. Guarino. 1975. Fertility of eggs produced on territories of vasectomized Red-winged Blackbirds. *Wilson Bulletin* 87:187–95.

Brenowitz, Eliot A. 1981. The effect of stimulus presentation sequence on the response of Red-winged Blackbirds in playback studies. *Auk* 98:355–60.

Burtt, Harold E., and Maurice L. Giltz. 1977. Seasonal directional patterns of movements and migrations of starlings and blackbirds in North America. *Bird-Banding* 48:259–71.

Chapman, Frank M. 1928. The nesting habits of Wagler's Oropendola (*Zarhynchus wagleri*) on Barro Colorado Island. *Bulletin American Museum of Natural History* 58:123–66.

Coble, Mary F. 1954. *Introduction to ornithological nomenclature.* Los Angeles: American Book Institute.

Comstock, John H. 1947. *An introduction to entomology.* New York: Comstock Publishing Company.

Crawford, Richard D. 1977. Breeding biology of year old and older female Red-winged and Yellow-headed blackbirds. *Wilson Bulletin* 89:73–80.

Cronmiller, James R., and Charles F. Thompson. 1980. Experimental manipulation of brood size in Red-winged Blackbirds. *Auk* 97:559–65.

Cutright, Noel J. 1973. *A bibliography on the Red-winged Blackbird.* Department of Natural Resources, New York State College of Agriculture and Life Sciences. Ithaca, New York: Cornell University. Mimeo.

Davie, Oliver. 1898. *Nests and eggs of North American birds.* Part 1. Columbus, Ohio: Landon Press.

Davis, Harold L. 1952. *Winds of morning.* Westport, Conn.: William Morrow, Greenwood Press.

Davis, John. 1954. Seasonal changes in bill length of certain passerine birds. *Condor* 56:142–49.

Dawson, William L. 1923. *The birds of California.* San Francisco: South Moulton Company.

Darling, F. Fraser. 1946. *A herd of red deer.* London: Oxford University Press.

DeGrazio, John W., Jerome F. Besser, Thomas J. DeCino, Joseph L. Guarino, and Edward W. Schafer, Jr. 1972. Protecting ripening corn from blackbirds by broadcasting 4-aminopyridine baits. *Journal of Wildlife Management* 36:1316–20.

DeHaven, Richard W. 1971. Blackbirds and the California rice crop. *The Rice Journal* 74:1–4.

Dickinson, Thomas E. 1981. The social significance of certain vocalizations of female Red-winged Blackbirds (*Agelaius phoeniceus*). Paper presented at the 99th Stated Meeting of the American Ornithologists' Union.

Dolbeer, Richard A. 1975. A comparison of two methods for estimating bird damage to sunflowers. *Journal of Wildlife Management* 39:802–6.

———. 1976. Reproductive rate and temporal spacing of nesting of Red-winged Blackbirds in upland habitat. *Auk:* 343–55.

———. 1978. Movement and migration patterns of Red-winged Blackbirds: a continental overview. *Bird-Banding* 49:17–34.

———. 1980. Blackbirds and corn in Ohio. *Resource Publication* 136, United States Department of the Interior, Fish & Wildlife Service. Washington, D.C.

———. 1981. Cost-benefit determination of blackbird damage control for corn-fields. *Wildlife Society Bulletin* 9:44–51.

———. 1982. Migration patterns for sex and age classes of blackbirds and star-lings. *Journal of Field Ornithology* 53: 28–46.

Dolbeer, Richard A., and Robert A. Stehn. 1979. Population trends of blackbirds and starlings in North America, 1966–76. *United States Fish and Wildlife Service, Special Scientific Report—Wildlife No. 214: 1–99.*

Dolbeer, Richard A., Paul B. Woronecki, Allen R. Stickley, Jr., and Stephen B. White. 1978. Agricultural impact of a winter population of blackbirds and starlings. *Wilson Bulletin* 90:31–44.

Dwight, Jonathon, Jr. 1900. The sequence of plumages and molts of the passer-ine birds of New York. *Annals New York Academy of Science.* 13:73–360.

Dyer, Mel I. 1975. The effects of Red-winged Blackbirds (*Agelaius phoeniceus* L.) on biomass production of corn grains (*Zea mays* L.). *Journal of Applied Ecology* 12:719–26.

"E., R." 1936. *The U.S. Biological Survey refuses protection to the blackbird. Forward into battle.* Year book of the Emergency Conservation Committee for 1935, Publication No. 53, New York.

Emlen, John T., Jr. 1958. Seminar on the breeding behaviour of waterfowl. Delta Waterfowl Research Station.

Eschmeyer, Paul H., and Van T. Harris, eds. 1974. *Bibliography of research publications of the Denver Wildlife Research Center 1941–72.* Reprinted from *Resource Publication No. 120, Bibliography of research publications of the United States Bureau of Sport Fisheries & Wildlife, 1928–72.*

Ewald, Paul E., and Sievert Rohwer. 1982. Effects of supplemental feeding on timing of breeding, clutch-size and polygyny in Red-winged Blackbirds *Agelaius phoeniceus. Journal of Animal Ecology* 51:429–50.

Ficken, Robert W. 1963. Courtship and agonistic behavior of the Common Grackle, *Quiscalus quiscula. Auk* 80:52–72.

Francis, William J. 1971. An evaluation of reported reproductive success in Red-winged Blackbirds. *Wilson Bulletin* 83:178–85.

———. 1973a. Blackbird nest placement and nesting success. *Wilson Bulletin* 85:86–87.

———. 1973b. Accuracy of census methods of territorial Red-winged Black-birds. *Journal of Wildlife Management* 37:98–102.

———. 1976. Micrometerology of a blackbird roost. *Journal of Wildlife Man-agement* 40:132–36.

Friedmann, Herbert. 1929. *The cowbirds.* Baltimore: C.C. Thomas.

Gilliard, Ernest T. 1958. *Living birds of the world.* New York: Doubleday and Company.

Greenwood, Hamilton. 1981. Sexual selection and the variable plumage charac-teristics of the subadult male Red-winged Blackbird. Paper presented at the 99th Stated Meeting of the American Ornithologists' Union.

Guarino, Joseph L., William F. Shake, and Edward W. Schafer, Jr. 1974. Reduc-ing bird damage to ripening cherries with methiocarb. *Journal of Wildlife Management* 38:338–42.

Hackett, Noel L. 1913. Notes on breeding birds of Agelaius phoeniceus. *Wilson Bulletin* 25:36–37.

Harke, Donald T., and Allen R. Stickley, Jr. 1968. Sensitive odometer aids road-side census of red-winged blackbirds. *Journal of Wildlife Management* 32:635–36.

Harding, Cheryl, and Brian K. Follett. 1979. Hormone changes triggered by aggression in a natural population of blackbirds. *Science* 203:918–20.

Hochbaum, H. Albert. 1944. *The Canvasback on a prairie marsh.* Washington, D.C.: American Wildlife Institute.

Holcomb, Larry C. 1968. Problems in the use of an embryocide to control passerine bird populations. *Transactions 33rd North American Natural Resources Conference,* pp. 307–16.

———. 1970. Prolonged incubation behavior of Red-winged Blackbirds incubating several egg sizes. *Behaviour* 35:74–83.

———. 1974. The question of possible surplus females in breeding Red-winged Blackbirds. *Wilson Bulletin* 86:177–79.

———1979. Response to foster nestlings by Red-winged Blackbirds *Agelaius phoeniceus* at different reproductive stages. *Wilson Bulletin* 91:434–40.

Holcomb, Larry C., and Gilbert Twiest. 1970. Growth rates and sex ratios of Red-winged Blackbird nestlings. *Wilson Bulletin* 82:294–303.

Howard, Ronald A., Jr. 1971. Territory frangibility and social structure in Red-winged Blackbirds. Abstract, American Society of Zoologists Annual Meeting December 26–31. *American Zoologist* 11:628.

Howard, H. Eliot. 1920. *Territory in bird life.* London: Murray.

———. 1929. *An introduction to the study of bird behaviour.* New York: Cambridge University Press.

Howard, Len. 1952. *Birds as individuals.* London: Collins.

Jackson, Jeffery J. 1971. Nesting ecology of the female Red-winged Blackbird. Ph.D. diss., Ohio State University.

Johnson, Ellen J., Richard A. Dolbeer, and Robert A. Stehn. 1982. Population status of blackbirds and starlings in North America, 1966–80: an update. *Denver Wildlife Research Center, Bird Damage Research Report No. 206:* 1–65.

Kendeigh, S. Charles. 1952. *Parental care and its evolution in birds.* Illinois Biological Monographs 22: 1–256.

Kennard, Frederick H. 1920. Notes on the breeding habits of the Rusty Blackbird in northern New England. *Auk* 37:412–22.

Knos, Carl. J., and Allen R. Stickley, Jr. 1974. Breeding Red-winged Blackbirds in captivity. *Auk* 91:808–16.

Lack, David, and John T. Emlen, Jr. 1939. Observations on breeding behavior in Tricolored Red-wings. *Condor* 41:225–30.

LaPrade, H. Renée, and H. B. Graves. 1982. Polygyny and female-female aggression in Red-winged Blackbirds (*Agelaius phoeniceus*). *American Naturalist* 120:135–38.

Larsen, James A. 1956. Wisconsin's renewable resources. *University of Wisconsin:* 1–160.

Laskey, Amelia R. 1933. A territory and mating study of mockingbirds. *Migrant* 4: 29–35.

Lenington, Sarah. 1980. Female choice and polygyny in Redwinged Blackbirds. *Animal Behavior* 28:347–61.

Linford, Gene H. 1935. The life history of the thick-billed red-winged blackbird, *Agelaius phoeniceus fortis* Ridgway, in Utah. Master's thesis, University of Utah Library.

Linsdale, Jean M. 1938. Environmental responses of vertebrates in the Great Basin. *American Midland Naturalist* 19:1–206.

Lowther, Peter E. 1975. Geographic and ecological variation in the family Icteridae. *Wilson Bulletin* 87:481–90.

McIllhenny, Edward A. 1937. Life history of the Boat-tailed Grackle in Louisiana. *Auk* 54:274–95.

Mayr, Ernst. 1941. Red-wing observations of 1940. *Proceedings of the Linnaean Society of New York* 52–53: 75–83.

Meanley, Brooke. 1962. Feeding behavior of the Red-winged Blackbird in the Dismal Swamp region in Virginia. *Wilson Bulletin* 74: 91–93.

———. 1964. Origin, structure, molt, and dispersal of a late summer Red-winged Blackbird population. *Bird-Banding* 35: 32–38.

———. 1965. The roosting behavior of the Red-winged Blackbird in the southern United States. *Wilson Bulletin* 77: 217–28.

———.1971. Blackbirds and the southern rice crop. *Resource Publication 100*, United States Department of the Interior, Fish & Wildlife Service, Washington, D.C.

———. 1975. The blackbird-starling roost problem. *Atlantic Naturalist* 30: 107–10.

Meanley, Brooke, and Gormon M. Bond. 1970. Molts and plumages of the Red-winged Blackbird with particular reference to fall migration. *Bird-Banding* 41: 22–27.

Meanley, Brooke, and Willis C. Royall, Jr. 1976. Nationwide estimates of blackbirds and starlings. *Proceedings Seventh Bird Control Seminar*, Bowling Green State University, Bowling Green, Ohio.

Meanley, Brooke, and John S. Webb. 1961. Distribution of winter Red-winged Blackbird populations on the Atlantic coast. *Bird-Banding* 32: 94–97.

———. 1965. Nationwide population estimates of blackbirds and starlings. *Atlantic Naturalist* 20: 189–91.

Mehner, John F. 1950. An ecological study of the eastern Red-winged Blackbird (*Agelaius phoeniceus*) at Pymatuning. Master's thesis, University of Pittsburgh.

Misikimen, Mildred. 1980. Red-winged Blackbirds: 1. Age-related epaulet color changes in captive females. 2. Pigmentation in epaulet of females. *Ohio Journal of Science* 80: 233–35, 236–39.

Morris, Lynn. 1975. Effect of blackened epaulets on the territorial behavior and breeding success of male Redwinged Blackbirds, *Agelaius phoeniceus*. *Ohio Journal of Science* 75: 168–76.

Mott, Donald F., Jerome F. Besser, Richard R. West, and John DeGrazio. 1972. Bird damage to peanuts and methods for alleviating the problem. *Proceedings 5th Vertebrate Pest Control Conference*, pp. 118–20.

Nero, Robert W. 1950. Notes on a Least Bittern nest and young. *Passenger Pigeon* 12: 3–8.

———. 1951. Red-wing, *Agelaius phoeniceus*, anting. *Auk* 68: 108.

———. 1954. Plumage aberrations of the Redwing (*Agelaius phoeniceus*). *Auk* 71: 137–55.

———. 1956. A behavior study of the Red-winged Blackbird. *Wilson Bulletin* 68: 5–37, 129–50.

———. 1960. Additional notes on the plumage of the Red-winged Blackbird. *Auk* 77: 298–305.

———. 1964. Comparative behavior of the Yellow-headed Blackbird, Red-winged Blackbird, and other icterids. *Wilson Bulletin* 75: 376–413.

Nero, Robert W., and John T. Emlen, Jr. 1951. An experimental study of territorial behavior in breeding Red-winged Blackbirds. *Condor* 53: 105–16.

Nice, Margaret M. 1937. Studies in the life history of the Song Sparrow. 1. A population study of the Song Sparrow. *Transactions of the Linnaean Society of New York* 4: 1–248.

———. 1943. Studies in the life history of the Song Sparrow. 2. The behavior of the Song Sparrow and other passerines. *Transactions of the Linnaean Society of New York* 6: 1–328.

———. 1950. Development of a redwing (*Agelaius phoeniceus*). *Wilson Bulletin* 62: 87–93.

Nuttall, Thomas. 1832. *A manual of the ornithology of the United States and of Canada.* Vol. 1. Cambridge, Mass.

Orians, Gordon H. 1960. Autumnal breeding in the Tricolored Blackbird. *Auk* 77: 379–98.

———. 1961. The ecology of blackbird (*Agelaius*) social systems. *Ecological Monographs* 31: 285–312.

———. 1969. On the evolution of mating systems in birds and mammals. *American Naturalist* 103: 589–603.

———. 1972. The adaptive significance of mating systems in the Icteridae. *Proceedings XV International Ornithological Congress*, pp. 389–98.

———. 1980. *Some adaptations of marsh-nesting blackbirds.* Princeton, N.J.: Princeton University Press.

Orians, Gordon H., and Gene Collier. 1963. Competition and blackbird social systems. *Evolution* 17: 449–59.

Orians, Gordon H., and Henry S. Horn. 1969. Overlap in food and foraging of four species of blackbirds in the potholes of central Washington. *Ecology* 50: 930–38.

Orians, Gordon H., and Gene M. Christman. 1968. A comparative study of the behavior of Red-winged, Tricolored, and Yellow-headed blackbirds. *University of California Publications in Zoology* 84. Berkeley and Los Angeles: University of California Press.

Orians, Gordon H., and Mary F. Willson. 1964. Interspecific territories of birds. *Ecology* 45: 736–45.

Payne, Robert B. 1969. Breeding seasons and reproductive physiology of Tricolored Blackbirds and Redwinged Blackbirds. *University of California Press Publications in Zoology* 90. Berkeley and Los Angeles: University of California Press.

Pearson, T. Gilbert, ed. 1936. *Birds of America.* Garden City, N.Y.: Garden City Publishing Company.

Peek, Frank W. 1971. Seasonal change in the breeding behavior of the Red-winged Blackbird. *Wilson Bulletin* 83: 383–95.

———. 1972. An experimental study of the territorial function of vocal and visual display in the male Red-winged Blackbird (*Agelaius phoeniceus*). *Animal Behavior* 20: 112–18.

Peek, Frank W., Edwin Franks, and Dennis Case. 1972. Recognition of nest, eggs, nest site, and young in female Red-winged Blackbirds. *Wilson Bulletin* 84: 243–49.

Peterson, Arnold, and Howard Young. 1950. A nesting study of the bronzed grackle. *Auk* 67: 466–76.

Peterson, Roger T. 1980. *A field guide to the birds.* Boston: Houghton Mifflin.

Picman, Jaroslav. 1980. Impact of marsh wrens on reproductive strategy of red-winged blackbirds. *Canadian Journal of Zoology* 51: 337–50.

Post, William. 1981. Biology of the Yellow-shouldered Blackbird—*Agelaius* on a tropical island. *Bull. Florida State Museum, Biological Sciences* 26(3): 135–202.

Proctor, Thomas. 1897. An unusual song of the red-winged blackbird. *Auk* 14: 319–20.

Rivinus, Edward F. 1976. Birds can be beautiful, but a million uninvited guests can spoil your whole winter and create some hard choices. *Smithsonian* 7.

Roberts, Thomas A., and James J. Kennelly. 1980. Variation in promiscuity among Red-winged Blackbirds. *Wilson Bulletin* 92: 110–12.

Roberts, Thomas S. 1909. A study of a breeding colony of yellow-headed blackbirds; including an account of the destruction of the entire progeny of the colony by some unknown natural agency. Auk 26: 371–89.

Robertson, Raleigh J. 1972. Optimal niche space of the red-winged blackbird (*Agelaius phoeniceus*). 1. Nesting success in marsh and upland habitat. *Canadian Journal of Zoology* 50: 247–63.

———. 1973. Optimal niche space of the Red-winged Blackbird. 3. Growth rate and food of nestlings in marsh and upland habitat. *Wilson Bulletin* 85: 209–22.

Robertson, Raleigh J., Patrick J. Weatherhead, Frank J.S. Phelan, Geoffrey L. Holroyd, and Nigel Lester. 1978. On assessing the economic and ecological impact of winter blackbird flocks. *Journal of Wildlife Management* 42: 53–60.

Schantz, William E. 1937. A nest-building male song-sparrow. *Auk* 54: 189–91.

Searcy, William A. 1979a. Male characteristics and pairing success in Red-winged Blackbirds. *Auk* 96:353–63.

———. 1979b. Female choice of mates: a general model for birds and its application to Red-winged Blackbirds (*Agelaius phoeniceus*). *American Naturalist* 114: 77–100.

———. 1979c. Male characteristics and pairing success in Red-winged Blackbirds. *Auk* 96: 353–63.

———. 1980. Morphological correlates of dominance in captive male Red-winged Blackbirds *Agelaius phoeniceus*. *Condor* 81: 417–20.

Searcy, William A., and John C. Wingfield. 1980. The effects of androgen and anti-androgen on dominance and aggressiveness in male Red-winged Blackbirds. *Hormones and Behavior* 14: 126–35.

Selander, Robert K., and Donald R. Giller. 1960. First-year plumages of the Brown-headed Cowbird and Red-winged Blackbird. *Condor* 62: 202–14.

Shipley, Frank S. 1979. Predation on Red-winged Blackbird eggs and nestlings. *Wilson Bulletin* 91: 426–33.

Short, Lester, L., Jr. 1969. A new species of blackbird (*Agelaius*) from Peru. *Occasional Papers of the Museum of Zoology* 36, Louisiana State University: 1–8.

Skowron, Carol, and Michael Kern. 1980. The insulation in nests of selected North American songbirds. *Auk* 97: 816–24.

Skutch, Alexander F. 1954. Life histories of Central American birds. *Cooper Ornithological Society, Pacific Coast Avifauna No. 31.*

Smith, Douglas G. 1972a. The red badge of rivalry. *Natural History* 81: 44–50.

———. 1972b. The role of the epaulets in the Red-winged Blackbird (*Agelaius phoeniceus*) social system. *Behaviour* 52: 251–68.

———. 1976. An experimental analysis of the function of Red-winged Blackbird song. *Behaviour* 56: 136–56.

———. 1979. Male singing ability and territory integrity in Red-winged Blackbirds (*Agelaius phoeniceus*). *Behaviour* 59: 193–206.

Smith, Douglas G., and Fiona A. Reid. 1979. Roles of the song repertoire in Redwinged Blackbirds. *Behavioral Ecology Sociobiology* 5: 279–90.

Smith, Douglas G., Fiona A. Reid, and Candace B. Breen. 1980. Stereotypy of some parameters of Red-winged Blackbird song. *Condor* 82: 259–66.

Smith, H. Muir, 1943. Size of breeding populations in relation to egg-laying and reproductive success in the eastern red-wing (*Agelaius p. phoeniceus*). *Ecology* 24: 183–207.

Smith, Lawrie B., and Ralph D. Bird. 1969. Autumn flocking habits of the Red-winged Blackbird in southern Manitoba. *Canadian Field-Naturalist* 83: 40–47.

Snelling, John C. 1968. Overlap in feeding habits of Redwinged Blackbirds and Common Grackles nesting in a cattail marsh. *Auk* 85: 560–85.

Soriano, Pablo S. 1931. Food habits and economic status of the Brewer and red-winged blackbirds. *California Fish and Game* 17: 361–85.

Sowls, Lyle K. *Prairie Ducks.* 1951. Harrisburg Pa.,: Stackpole Company; and Washington, D.C.: Wildlife Management Institute.

Stickley, Allen R., Jr., and Joseph L. Guarino. 1972. A repellent for protecting corn seed from blackbirds and crows. *Journal of Wildlife Management* 36: 150–52.

Stickley, Allen R., Jr., and Robert T. Mitchell, John L. Seubert, Charles R. Ingram, and Mel I. Dyer. 1976. Large-scale evaluation of blackbird frightening agent 4-amino-pyridine in corn. *Journal of Wildlife Management* 40: 126–31.

Stone, Charles P. 1972. Blackbirds versus corn. *The Farm Quarterly* 27: 61.

Stone, Charles P., and Glenn A. Hood. 1979. Extent, costs, and trends in control of plant pests, vertebrates. Pages 218–32 in W. B. Ennis., Jr. (ed.), *Introduction to Crop Protection.* Madison, Wis.: American Agronomy and Crop Science Society of America.

Stone, Charles P., and Donald F. Mott. 1973a. Bird damage to ripening field corn in the United States, 1971. *United States Department of the Interior, Fish and Wildlife Service, Wildlife Leaflet No. 505.*

———. 1973b. Bird damage to sprouting corn in the United States. *United States Department of the Interior, Fish and Wildlife Service, Special Scientific Report—Wildlife No. 173.*

Stone, Charles P., Donald F. Mott, Jerome F. Besser, and John W. DeGrazio. 1972. Bird damage to corn in the United States in 1970. *Wilson Bulletin* 84: 101–5.

Stone, Charles P., Donald F. Mott, James E. Forbes, and Charles P. Breidenstein. 1973. Bird damage to field corn in New York, 1971. *New York Fish and Game Journal* 20: 68–73.

Tinbergen, Niko. 1939. The behaviour of the Snow Bunting in spring. *Transactions of the Linnaean Society of New York* 5: 1–94.

Tyler, Barry M.J., and Lyn W. Kannenberg. 1980. Blackbird (*Agelaius phoeniceus*) damage to ripening corn *Zea mays* in Ontario, Canada. *Canadian Journal of Zoology* 58: 469–72.

Tyler, Winsor M. 1923. Courting orioles and blackbirds from the female bird's eyeview. *Auk* 40: 696–97.

Van Tyne, Josselyn, and Andrew J. Berger. 1959. *Fundamentals of ornithology.* New York: John Wiley and Sons.

Verner, Jared. 1964. Evolution of polygamy in the Long-billed Marsh Wren. *Evolution* 18: 252–61.

Wallace, George J. 1955. *An introduction to ornithology.* Toronto: Macmillan of Canada.

Weatherhead, Patrick J. 1981a. The dynamics of Red-winged Blackbird populations at four late summer roosts in Quebec. *Journal of Field Ornithology* 52: 222–27.

———. 1981b. Coming home to roost. *Nature Canada* 10: 38–43.

Weatherhead, Patrick J., and J. Roger Bider. 1979. Management options for blackbird problems in agriculture. *Phytoprotection* 60: 145–55.

Weatherhead, Patrick J., and Raleigh J. Robertson. 1977a. Male behavior and female recruitment in the Red-winged Blackbird. *Wilson Bulletin* 89: 583–92.

———. 1977b. Harem size, territory quality and reproductive success in the Red-winged Blackbird (*Agelaius phoeniceus*). *Canadian Journal of Zoology* 55: 1261–67.

Weatherhead, Patrick J., J. Roger Bider, and Robert G. Clarke. 1980. Surfactants and the management of Red-winged Blackbirds in Quebec. *Phytoprotection* 61: 39–47.

Weatherhead, Patrick J., Hamilton Greenwood, Stephen H. Tinker, and J. Roger Bider. 1980. Decoy traps and the control of blackbird populations. *Phytoprotection* 61: 65–71.

Weatherhead, Patrick J., and Raleigh J. Robertson. 1979. Offspring quality and the polygyny threshold: 'the sexy son hypothesis.' *American Naturalist* 113: 201–8.

Webb, John S., and Brooke Meanley. 1973. Distribution and ecology of blackbird and starling roosts in eastern United States. *United States Fish & Wildlife Service Progress Report, November 1973.* Mimeo. p. 41.

Welty, Joel C. 1962. *The life of birds.* Philadelphia: W.B. Saunders Company.

Wetmore, Alexander. 1920. Observations on the habits of birds at Lake Burford, New Mexico. *Auk* 37: 393–412.

Wiens, John A. 1965. Behavioral interactions of Red-winged Blackbirds and Common Grackles on a common breeding ground. *Auk* 82: 356–74.

Williams, J. Fred. 1940. The sex ratio in nestling eastern red-wings. *Wilson Bulletin 52: 267–77.*

Williams, Laidlaw. 1952. Breeding behavior of the Brewer Blackbird. *Condor* 54: 3–47.

Wing, Leonard W. 1956. *Natural history of birds.* New York: Ronald Press Company.

Wood, Harold B. 1938. Nesting of Red-winged Blackbirds. *Wilson Bulletin* 50: 143–44.

Woronecki, Paul P., Robert A. Stehn, and Richard A. Dolbeer. 1980. Compensatory response of maturing corn kernels following simulated damage by birds. *Journal of Applied Ecology* 17: 737–46.

Yasukawa, Ken. 1978. Aggressive tendencies and levels of a graded display: factor analysis of response to song playback in the Redwinged Blackbird (*Agelaius phoeniceus*). *Behavioral Biology* 23: 446–59.

———. 1979. Territory establishment in Red-winged Blackbirds: importance of aggressive behavior and experience. *Condor* 81: 258–64.

———. 1981. Song and territory defense in the Red-winged Blackbird. *Auk* 98: 185–87.

Index